FOR THE RECORD II

More Encouraging Words for Ordinary Catholics

——— ℰℐ ———

Also by J. Ronald Knott

An Encouraging Word
Renewed Hearts, Renewed Church
The Crossroads Publishing Co., 1995

One Heart at a Time
Renewing the Church in the New Millennium
Sophronismos Press, 1999

Sunday Nights
Encouraging Words for Young Adults
Sophronismos Press, 2000

Diocesan Priests in the Archdiocese of Louisville
Archdiocese of Louisville Vocation Office, 2001

Religious Communities in the Archdiocese of Louisville
Archdiocese of Louisville Vocation Office, 2002

For the Record: Encouraging Words for Ordinary Catholics
Sophronismos Press, 2003

Intentional Presbyterates: Claiming Our Common Sense of Purpose as Diocesan Priests
Sophronismos Press, 2003

From Seminarian to Priest: Managing the Transition
Sophronismos Press, 2005

FOR THE RECORD II
More Encouraging Words for Ordinary Catholics

Rev. J. Ronald Knott

Sophronismos Press   Louisville, Kentucky

FOR THE RECORD II
More Encouraging Words for Ordinary Catholics

First Printing: October 2004
ISBN 0-9668969-4-7

Printed in the United States of America

Morris Publishing
3212 East Highway 30
Kearney, NE 68847
1-800-650-7888

To the many ordinary Catholics whose enduring faith has kept me in the priesthood for almost thirty-five years and made it the joy of my life.

Acknowledgments

I would like to thank Mr. Joseph Duerr, editor of *The Record,* our archdiocesan newspaper, for giving me the opportunity to write these weekly columns. I also thank Mr. Glenn Rutherford for editing these columns each week and for giving me valuable advice along the way. I would like to offer a special thanks to Ms. Lori Massey for formatting these columns into a book. Last of all, I would like to thank the many, many people who have responded so favorably to these columns each week.

I write these few words to you
... to encourage you never to
let go of the true grace of
God to which I bear witness.

I Peter 5:12

PREFACE

Believe It or Not, It's Column 100

The community read it and were delighted with the encouragement it gave them. Acts 15:31

I can't believe it, but this is my 100th "Encouraging Word" column. I have been writing these for two years.

In general, the response has been overwhelmingly positive, more than I could have imagined. I am regularly stopped by people in groceries, restaurants and on the street. I get a whole lot of mail.

What they usually say is some version of, "It's down to earth" and "It's something that touches real life." I am not an academic, nor do I claim to be. I am a pastor at heart, and the whole purpose of these columns is to encourage the ordinary Catholic in the pew.

One experience stands out above all else. One night, when I was feeling "down," I decided to walk to the White Castle for coffee. As I sat there brooding, a large group of what appeared to be 12- to 13-year-olds invaded the place. I prepared myself to finish and leave when one of them yelled out, "Are you a priest?" (These days, you never know what will come after that question.) I cautiously answered, "Yes."

All of a sudden two or three yelled out, "I told you it was him." Then they went on to say that they recognized me from my picture at the top of my column in *The Record*. Two or three said together, "We read it all the time." Another said his mother reads it to him or leaves in on the refrigerator.

That experience alone made it all worthwhile.

Even though the response has been overwhelmingly positive, I have had a handful of critics. Most of the criticism comes from those who were upset by what they perceived as my questioning of certain liturgical intricacies and for being too generous with compassion. Some have simply missed the point or failed to get the tongue-in-cheek humor.

Someone described John the Baptist as both "critical and committed." People who are not committed to the church have no right to criticize it, but those of us who are committed have a right and sometimes even a duty to be critical.

Anyone who swallows everything going on in the church today — hook, line and sinker — does the church, I believe, a disservice. I agree with Cardinal Karol Wojtyla, now Pope John Paul II, who said in 1969, "Conformism means death for any community; a loyal opposition is a necessity in any community." The crucial word, of course, is "loyal."

I have been a committed Roman Catholic since I was born. I have been a seminarian or priest since the age of 14. I believe my commitment to the church comes across loud and clear in my columns and in my life — at least I want it to. But that does not make me blind, deaf and dumb. I care enough to criticize once in a while, and that, I believe, is a good thing.

September 30, 2004

Table of Contents

In the Comfort of our Guardian Angels

See, I am sending an angel before you, to guard you on the way and bring you to the place I have prepared. Exodus 23:20

Do you believe in signs? When I was typing the Scripture quote above, a TV character on the screen behind me said something about somebody being "surrounded by angels." Did I just experience one of those serendipitous moments that has happened to me repeatedly when I write? I believe so.

I am not one of those sentimentalists who just discovered the new-age "angel craze." In fact, I have not been "into" angels since I was in the first and second grades. Back then, I believed strongly in angels. I found that belief very comforting. One of the most memorable things hanging on the front wall of my classroom back then was that beautiful picture of a "guardian angel" escorting a little boy and girl across a rickety bridge over a roaring stream. Since I felt that my life was precarious in those days, I always found that picture very consoling.

After that, I guess I believed in angels, but I never thought about them all that much. That is, until my mother was dying of cancer. In the hours before her death, she was convinced that there were angels standing at the foot of her bed, as well as all her deceased brothers and sisters. She was adamant about it, even to the point of telling us they had beautiful purple robes. She normally hated the color purple.

I sort of dismissed it as the hallucinations of a dying woman until we got to her funeral and heard the words of the Rite of Commendation when our pastor prayed the ancient prayer: "May the angels lead you into paradise; may the martyrs come to welcome you and take you to the holy city, the new and eternal Jerusalem. May choirs of angels welcome you and lead you to the bosom of Abraham; and where Lazarus is poor no longer may you find eternal rest."

Did she see something we didn't see?

In a world that tends to believe in only things seen, in a church that is more and more rational in its religious practice, angels are often dismissed as a sentimental creation that only the Hallmark Company still embraces. No so. The Catechism of the Catholic Church says that "the existence of spiritual, non-corporeal beings that Sacred Scripture usually calls 'angels' is a truth of faith. ... The witness of Scripture is as clear as the unanimity of Tradition. These servants and messengers of God surround human beings with their watchful care and intercession."

Today is the feast of the Guardian Angels. Is this belief only for children? In a way, yes. Did Jesus not say, "Unless you change and become like little children, you will not enter the Kingdom of God?" It is pretty dumb to be so smart that you lose your childlike faith. A guardian angel is still a comforting thought, no matter how old I get.

October 2, 2003

2

The Mistake of Punishing the Innocent

Then Abraham said to God, "Will you sweep away the innocent along with the guilty?" Genesis 19:23

The worst spanking I ever got when I was a child growing up in Rhodelia, Ky., was over a bunch of apples. I might have been 5 or 6 years old.

Junius Greenwell, our neighbor, had a big apple tree in the field next to his house. When the apples were ripe, we asked him if we could have some of them. He said, "Yes, of course, take all you want."

As children, we unfortunately took him literally. We rolled a 55-gallon drum up to the tree and stripped it of its apples, without the faintest idea of how we would get it home or what we would do with all that fruit.

The short of it was, Junius Greenwell was extremely upset and told my Dad when Dad got home from work. Probably overly tired, my Dad went into a rage and spanked all of us kids. His words were similar to these: "Since I don't know who is guilty and who is not, you're all going to get it."

And so we did. As far as I know, that was my first experience of seeing the innocent punished for guilt by association.

I have been hearing a rumor here and there that some Catholics plan to boycott this year's Catholic Services Appeal as a way of punishing troubled priests and those who "protected" them. I hope they don't carry through on this threat because if they do, they will be punishing all the wrong people.

The Catholic Services Appeal funds such programs as Catholic Charities, which works to help refugees, the elderly, couples seeking to adopt and others. The Catholic Services Appeal also helps train parish volunteers in religious education, liturgy and youth ministry. It helps fund this newspaper, television broadcasting and outreaches on subjects such as marriage preparation, divorce, religious vocations, home mission work, bereavement and mental illness. My own office, the Vocation Office, which tries to promote all vocations, especially vocations to priesthood and religious life, has already been cut back dramatically.

Withholding support for the Catholic Services Appeal will not punish the offending priests or the bishop as much as it will hundreds of innocent people who had nothing to do with this crisis. The work of the church in carrying out the mission of Christ himself, including the healing of those who have been hurt, must go on no matter how frustrated and angry we are at those few who have committed these crimes or those who have dealt with them. Hurting those who are innocent is not a good way of expressing that anger and frustration.

Even though I had my own salary frozen because of this demoralizing crisis, I hope to give more, not less, this year. I also hope that most Catholics will do the same, not for the sake of the guilty but for the sake of the innocent.

October 9, 2003

There Can be Comfort in Living Alone

When he had sent them away, he went up on
the mountain to pray, remaining there alone
as evening drew on. Matthew 14:23-24

This week I send a very special greeting to those of you who live
alone as I do. I'm hopeful that you made it over the suicidal hump a
few years back and have come to love being alone without being
lonely.

I must admit that living alone takes some getting used to, and not
everyone gets to the point of comfort and peace. For some it is a
terrifying, unwanted and bitter daily experience.

When it comes to living alone, my trial by fire came in 1975 when I
moved into the basement apartment of St. Peter Church in
Monticello, Ky., as the first resident priest of Wayne County, down
on the Tennessee border.

The church was in the middle of an open field on the edge of
town. The only small window had an air conditioner in it. I had a used
bed; a battered nightstand; the world's ugliest lamp; a warped, green
kitchen table and two chairs. There were seven parishioners, and
the church had $90 in the bank.

The apartment was like a tomb. You could not hear a sound. I
remember my first night, trying to go to sleep and keep from crying. I
remember lying there in the dark, half praying and half cursing, mut-
tering to myself: "This is a very bad idea! What have I gotten myself
into?" Groundhog Day took on special significance during those
years.

People who live alone are no longer just "home missionaries," freaks, old-maid school teachers, unibombers, the ugly and the unloved. According to the 2000 census, people who live alone now account for one-fourth of the grown-up population, outnumbering married couples with children for the first time. There are about 27 million of us in this country.

Elderly people living alone comprise close to 30.5 percent of all older households, with women accounting for almost 78 percent of all those elderly who live by themselves. Most suffer in silence and look forward to those occasional, often unpredictable, visits from family members and a dwindling list of old friends.

I visit a 95-year-old widow every Friday on my day off. It's hard enough to live alone when you choose it, but harder still when you have no other real choice. My heart goes out to them.

There are advantages in living alone. You can eat moldy food and no one will stop you; you can leave the bed unmade and no one will see it; you can go to bed and get up when you want and no one will correct you; you can talk to yourself and no one will report you. But the biggest advantage of all may be finding yourself praying out loud and often.

In the end, living alone is a trade-off. Now that we have gotten used to it, some of us would find it hard to go back.

October 16, 2003

Sometimes We Need to "Clean House"

Stop turning my Father's house into a marketplace. John 2

In a moment of great humility, something rare for our church at that time, the bishops of Vatican II admitted that the church is "semper reformanda" — "always in need of reform." The human side of the church, just as all human organizations, has a tendency to fall into sin and decay and must be called back to fidelity, over and over again, as it moves through history.

In the above reading, which depicts a dramatic and public gesture of outrage, Jesus' anger boils over. It is very important to remember that the anger of Jesus was not directed at people who sinned or failed in all their everyday ways. His anger was directed at those who controlled religion and used it to abuse simple people.

He had pity and compassion on the outcasts, the sick and sinner, but he was outraged at what had happened at the hands of their leaders to the religion he loved. In some of the most blunt words from the mouth of Jesus ever recorded, he called them "snakes, fakes and frauds." He called the places of worship "whitewashed tombs ... all clean and pretty on the outside, but filled with stench and rot on the inside."

It is important to note that Jesus was not against organized religion, but what these people had done to organized religion. As this Gospel story tells us, he did not come to tear down the temple; he simply came to clean house. The temple had become a marketplace, and they were making a profit in every corner of it.

It is sad that many people never see beyond the packaging when it comes to religion. They see only the earthenware jar and never the treasure it holds. The purpose of religion is to serve, not be served. The purpose of organized religion is the transformation of people, not using people to serve organized religion.

It is also sad that many people naively assume that organized religion is evil simply because it has gotten off track here and there in history. Jesus was clear that he did not come to destroy organized religion but to lead it back to its original purpose.

Without organized religion, we would not have the sacred Scriptures, we would be split into millions of personal opinions and small little cults, and we would not have a way to offer support to other believers around the world. Yes, the church may need a good "house cleaning" every now and then, but the organization of the church is always needed.

As Kenneth Woodward has pointed out, for the last 30 or 40 years people have operated out of a romantic notion that all the ills of the church reside with the institution — so that if only we could reform it, we ourselves would be better Christians. The truth quite often is the other way around. The institution will get better when each one of us is reformed and transformed.

October 23, 2003

Being a Parent is Really Hard Work

Whoever welcomes this little child on my account welcomes me, and whoever welcomes me welcomes him who sent me; for the least one among you is the greatest. Luke 9:48

When I see parents struggling with their kids, I sometimes wonder what my kids would have been like and what kind of parent I would have been. When I do, I usually shudder.

It is not easy being a priest, but parenting appears to be a whole lot harder. Parents are the real heroes, because parenting takes the selflessness of Mother Teresa, the patience of Job and the resources of a small country.

Since I am not a parent myself, I am only a parent watcher. I have four sisters and two brothers, and I have watched my 20 nieces and nephews grow. I have watched parents in church, in grocery stores and driving down the street in their mini-vans. I have held the hands of many parents who have had their hearts broken by the behavior of their own children and have kept loving them anyway. They all have my deepest respect and admiration.

I have witnessed a parent's incredible love. When I was a child growing up in the country in the 1950s, we didn't have a lot. Money was tight, and nothing went to waste. When my mother fried chicken, she fried every part of it, including the chicken's back, which she ate. As a child, I actually thought she loved chicken backs. I was much older before it dawned on me that she did that out of love. She did that so that we, her children, could have the best parts.

I have witnessed a parent's exasperation. One of my sisters, when she had three teenaged boys at the same time, used to say, "Now I know why some species eat their young at birth." A friend told me recently about his son, who was on a full scholarship, dropping out of college and coming back home with only a semester left before graduation. We all read in the newspaper recently about the handsome young man who died of a party-drug overdose.

I have witnessed a parent's selflessness. If they are lucky, parenting is a minimum of 20 years of "give, give, give." I say "lucky" because today many parents now face the prospect of having their children move back in, sometimes with a couple of kids of their own. Just when they think it is over, they find themselves parenting yet again.

I have also witnessed the pride that some parents have in seeing their children do well, sometimes beyond their wildest expectations. I see those children unfolding as talented and generous young adults in my ministry at Bellarmine University. You see this parent-pride most dramatically on graduation days.

My "encouraging word" today goes out to all you parents who have the awesome vocation of raising children. Pat yourselves on the back and know that you, especially, are doing God's work.

October 30, 2003

We Must Learn to Share God Peacefully

"Whoever is not against us is for us." Mark 9:40

Oh, how the world has changed. Even to say something like that dates me, but it is true.

When I was growing up, it was considered a sin to attend a non-Catholic church service without the explicit permission of your pastor. When you were given that permission, usually to attend a funeral or wedding of a non-Catholic relative, it was given with a warning — you can go, but don't participate.

Why? The fear was that if you went, they would try to convert you out of the true church, and if you showed any enthusiasm for what they said or did, you were condoning heresy, and that was a big sin.

Protestants did pretty much the same to us, even to the point of doubting whether we were even a "Christian" church or not, an attitude that prevails in some places even today. It is all part of pain left over from that messy divorce we know as the Reformation of the 16th century.

Oh, how the world has changed. Even the conservative Pope John Paul II has visited synagogues, mosques and Protestant churches throughout his pontificate. These are just a few examples of the many ecumenical and interfaith breakthroughs many of us now take for granted, breakthroughs that were made possible at the Second Vatican Council not too many years ago.

In the Gospel, John complains to Jesus that he saw someone outside their group using Jesus' name to drive out demons, and since that person was not part of the group, he ought to be stopped. In another place, John and his brother James volunteer to "call down fire from heaven to burn up" some Samaritans for snubbing their group. Like Moses rebuking the young Joshua for his similar exclusionary thinking in the Book of Numbers, Jesus rebukes the young John for his "them and us" thinking.

We live in a different world today than we did even 50 years ago, much of which is a result of mass communication and migration. Religions are being thrown together like never before, both literally and virtually. Our in-laws, neighbors, fellow citizens and friends now represent a variety of religions. We continue to fear what we do not know, and when we are afraid and ignorant, we do some crazy things to each other.

All these religions must learn to not only share this earth peacefully, but also to share God peacefully. Even though Roman Catholicism is the largest Christian group, only 32.4 percent of the world is Christian.

We Catholics must find a way to be consciously Christian, deliberately Catholic, and seriously ecumenical and interfaith at the same time. This does not imply that one religion is as good as another or that all are equally right or true. It simply implies that every human being has the right to follow his or her own conscience, and that God can do good things in other religions and even outside organized religion altogether.

November 6, 2003

Shake It Off and Move On

When people will not receive you, leave that town and shake its dust from your feet as a testimony against them. Luke 9

When I was newly ordained, I was full of enthusiasm to finally begin ministry after 12 years of seminary preparation. Not too long into my first assignment, I found myself as the first Catholic priest to live in Wayne County, Ky. I was one of eight Catholics in that whole county.

Catholics back then were a feared minority. Catholicism was looked on as a cult, much like the Moonies. My enthusiasm and good intentions were constantly coming up against a tangible prejudice that I could not understand.

I had anti-Catholic homilies preached about me personally on the radio by people I had never met. One preacher told his radio audience that "if they had prayed harder, those Catholics would not have come."

I had a Sunday morning radio program for a while, but I was thrown off the air while I was on vacation because "some ministers objected." Another preacher told his audience that "we can do without Rev. Knott and his kind."

At first I reacted like the apostle John when Jesus and his disciples were snubbed by some Samaritans on a trip to Jerusalem. "Lord, would you like for us to call down fire from heaven and burn them up?"

One day, when I was especially hurt by their rejection, I came across this passage and made a decision to react differently. I chose neither to "call down fire from heaven and burn them up" nor "shake their dust from my feet and move to another town." I decided to stand my ground and kill them with kindness.

For five years I deliberately looked for ways to affirm other ministers in their ministry and to look for ways to be as positive as I could toward the other churches of that community. It took a while, but when I left five years later, the local paper wrote a large, glowing, front-page article on my years of service to that community.

It seems that I am running into a lot of people these days who are struggling with loss, disappointment and rejection. In their anger, they battle the urge to fight back, to get even, and even to hate. Their anger is a counterproductive emotional cancer that eats at their soul. It's as though they're saying, "I'll get you by hurting me." There is another way, a more Christ-like way: "Shake it off and move on!"

Recently, I experienced a painful round of disappointment and loss. I know that for my own good, I have to shake it off and move on, so I have set a goal for myself: let go, forgive everybody, be thankful, leave well, move on, open myfs arms and believe that the best is yet to come. Leave or stay — love them anyway. This is my advice to any of you who have suffered a major loss or a serious bout of disappointment.

November 20, 2003

Facing the Responsibility to Make Wise Choices

Test everything. Retain what is good.
Refrain from every kind of evil.
1 Thessalonians 5:21-22

Americans are so used to having choices that we forget just how fortunate we are. A "buffet table" might just be the perfect symbol for our culture.

We are known around the world for having unlimited choices, but we are also known for making some very poor choices. Simply having the freedom to choose does not guarantee making good decisions. We may have a right to choose, but we also have a responsibility to choose wisely because our choices, good or bad, have an effect on ourselves and others.

This is exactly what Paul tells the Thessalonians. He tells them to wait for the coming of the Lord, living not as victims of their own addictions and compulsions, but intentionally, on purpose and selectively. To do that, he offers some timely advice: Look before you leap; don't fall for everything you see or hear. And after you have checked it out, keep what is good and reject the rest.

Paul's words to the Thessalonians are words to us as well. We live in a society, and a time in history, when personal "choice" is seen as a "right." Just as freedom must be paired with responsibility, wisdom must be paired with choice. Stupidity paired with choice spells disaster. In other words, we may have the freedom to choose, but we also have the responsibility to choose wisely. For instance:

• We are free to eat what we want, but when we eat anything and everything in sight, just because it is there, we should not expect to have a slim, healthy body.

• Sexual activity of any kind is readily available, but if we engage in irresponsible sexual activity, we should not be surprised by disastrous consequences — sexually transmitted diseases, unwanted pregnancies and ruined relationships.

• We are free to experiment with illicit drugs, but we should know the devastating consequences of addiction, which include disasters in finances, relationships, health and spirituality.

• We are free to accept multiple credit cards, but if we use them without the resources to pay for the things we have charged, we will pay dearly and choke off other possibilities for years to come.

• We have the freedom to vote, but not exercising that right regularly could lead to the loss of that right altogether.

• We have the freedom to marry and have children, but we must also be ready to accept not only the advantages, but also the personal limitations that go with such commitments.

Failing to count the cost before acting will hurt us and others for years to come. Yes, we have the right to choose, but we must also be willing to accept responsibility for our bad choices.

Even though Paul's advice is centuries old, it is still right on target and useful today: examine things carefully; look before you leap; everything that glitters is not gold; test everything; keep what is truly good and reject every kind of evil.

November 27, 2003

16

Remembering the Needs of our Rural Parishes

Can anything good come out of Nazareth? John 1:46

We have all heard the expression "out of sight, out of mind." This expression can certainly be used in reference to our priests, religious sisters and brothers, deacons and lay ministers heroically serving in the home missions of our diocese.

I still remember an occasion when this expression came true for me when I was a newly ordained priest. I had been serving for a year or two down in the southeastern corner of our diocese. I came to Louisville to attend a meeting. When I entered the room, one of our priests asked me what diocese I was from. In a chilly voice I answered, "Your diocese, Father."

Raised in a rural parish and having served in four rural and mission parishes, I have become sensitized to the urban orientation of the Roman Catholic church.

In its infancy the church was Jerusalem-centered. During its great missionary expansion, the apostles went out to establish churches in the major cities of the Roman Empire. With the conversion of the Emperor Constantine, the head of the congregation in a particular city became its bishop. Like the political structure of the Roman Empire, the church became city-centered and took its political structure as its model. This movement has characterized much of our church ever since.

The church in America originally operated this way. Where people established themselves, the officials and structure of the church followed. For many years, trained Protestant and Catholic clergy remained mainly in the eastern cities of America. Recoiling from frontier conditions, serious missionary efforts came only after some one hundred years, and when they did, Baptist and Methodist structures were more in keeping with the rural way of life.

This was true of the Roman Catholic church. During the great immigration period of the early 19th century, when so many Catholics entered this country, the immigrants tended to settle into cities. The clergy, limited in number, became so absorbed in meeting the spiritual needs of these people that there was little time for expanding into rural areas.

Though the history of the Roman Catholic church in our archdiocese began with the establishment of several rural parishes, by the early 1900s one of our bishops refused to accept any more seminarians because "we have no place to use them," even though 90 percent of the diocese had no Catholic presence. Other than a big push in the 1970s to establish the Southern Kentucky Missions, the Catholic church in Kentucky is still very much urban-centered.

In the last few years, because of the priest shortage and scandal payouts, the church has entered a period of cutbacks, downsizing and mergers that once again has raised the possibility that the needs of the urban church will overpower the needs of the rural church. Trying to maintain what we have has overpowered our need to be an expanding, evangelizing church, and our rural and missionary parishes stand to suffer most.

December 4, 2003

Hoping to use Words that Move People to Act

Samuel grew up, and the Lord was with him, not permitting any word of his to be without effect. 1 Samuel 3:19

One of my most memorable uncles was Uncle Sam. He and Aunt Eula were farmers. You couldn't meet two people who were more Christian. They were not the so-called overly religious type; they just loved God by being good to people. All their many nieces and nephews have a soft spot in their hearts for Uncle Sam and Aunt Eula.

Uncle Sam liked to talk. Everything he did was important to him, and he wanted to talk about it. It took a room full of people, taking turns, to listen to Uncle Sam.

It occurred to me the other day that I must have a lot of Uncle Sam in me. Preaching, teaching and lecturing is what I do for a living. I preach every weekend, often at as many as five Masses. Just in the last six years, I have preached in more than 75 parishes, not to mention preaching weekly at Bellarmine University. I have preached more than 50 parish missions, not to mention an untold number of retreats, conferences and conventions. That's a lot of talking. I even had a dream where God appeared to me late one Sunday night and said, "Ron, shut up!"

I probably talk more than my uncle Sam ever did, but what I wish is that I could be more like Samuel in the old testament. When Samuel spoke, "the Lord did not permit any word of his to be without effect." His words moved people. That is what every preacher and spiritual writer dreams about.

When I got up the nerve to start this column, I knew what I wanted to do, but I didn't know if I could do it. I wanted my words to encourage ordinary Catholics during this time of trial for our church. The feedback has been more affirming than I could have ever imagined. I get a kick out of running into total strangers at the grocery or gas station and discussing their reaction to something I wrote. I especially like to hear that people often clip these columns and send them to their children, relatives and friends.

What has been most affirming is when people tell me that they changed their minds about something: such as reconciling with a family member, deciding not to boycott the CSA or looking at an old problem in a new way.

At the end of this year, I will be leaving my post as vocation director. I will take a needed sabbatical until spring. At that time I will come back and take another assignment. While I will be relieved of many of the responsibilities that I have had, I plan to continue to write this column, because so many people have told me that they look forward to reading it each week. Besides, I will need something legitimate and constructive to do while I rest and prepare myself for the last leg of the race before retirement.

December 11, 2003

Chronicling the Decline of Santa Claus

Today is born our Savior, Christ the Lord. Luke 2:11

Ever since St. Nicholas changed his name to Santa Claus, he has been going downhill fast. How did he sink so far?

Nicholas started off as a rich young man from Turkey who ended up a becoming a kindly bishop. Dressed in a red cope, miter and crosier, he was known for his love of children and his determination to use his inheritance doing anonymous works of charity.

Seventeenth-century Dutch Protestants helped turn him into a married ex-priest living at the North Pole. Instead of being a holy bishop presiding over a diocese, he ended up presiding over a gang of workaholic elves.

Obviously, he married without being "laicized." Why else would he have been banished to such a God-forsaken place as the North Pole?

It must have been a traumatic career change. He ended up with a serious eating disorder and a possible drinking problem that turned him into a rotund bag of bad cholesterol with a bad case of rosacea.

Just when you thought he could not sink any lower, he is now starring in a new "adult" movie with an R rating called "Bad Santa." For those who think foul-mouthed drunks and vulgar rudeness are funny, this movie promises to be a huge hit. The reviews use words such as "demented, twisted, gloriously rude, rancid, vulgar and unreasonably funny."

So far, no one has raised any serious questions about his obsession with children, his enslaving of small animals to carry loads heavier than any UPS jet, or his penchant for "breaking and entering" homes all over the world. Of course, there is always next year.

St. Nicholas, the compassionate bishop, is not the only one to lose at this time of year. Even Jesus is being nudged out by elves, reindeer and kittens in Christmas stockings.

Instead of Jesus' birth being central, Christmas has become a frenzy of buying — buying things that people usually don't need, for people they don't like, with money they don't have. Just recently a mob of shoppers, rushing like a herd of charging elephants, trampled the first woman in line, knocking her unconscious. No wonder so many are left disappointed and in debt and the suicide rate spikes right after Christmas.

Before you dismiss me as a grinch, let me assure you that I love Christmas. My point is that it takes a lot of imagination and determination these days to "keep Christ in Christmas." Since I am single and my life is so different from that of many people, I am reluctant to give practical suggestions, but here is one. Keep it simple. Do less, not more. Take a little of the time you saved and go on a one-hour retreat. Take a long walk by yourself, visit an empty church or take a long soak in a quiet tub and try to remember what Christmas is really all about.

December 18, 2003

A Christmas that Taught Something New

Darkness covers the earth and thick clouds cover the peoples: but upon you the Lord shines and over you appears his glory. Isaiah 60:3

I just went through my 59th Christmas. Every one of them has been different. Every one of them has taught me something new, including this last one.

In December I bounced between laughing and crying like I have done every Christmas before. When all was said and done, it was a very inspiring Christmas. I felt closer to God, and I never needed this more than the end of this past year.

Over the last month alone, I was involved in a series of events that only a priest is lucky enough to experience. I celebrated the funeral of a feisty 100-year-old woman who befriended me when I was pastor of the Cathedral. I heard the confessions of retired nuns, holy women, who taught and nursed for 50-plus years without enough recognition or appreciation. I attended a prayer day with a room full of demoralized priests, not knowing where to turn except to God.

I celebrated Mass with 500 wonderful young women at Assumption High School. I heard the confessions of a wonderful youth group at St. Elizabeth Ann Seton parish and marveled at their goodness. I filled in for Father Joe Rankin at St. Francis of Assisi parish while he was on sabbatical. St. Francis is an example of what a good pastor and a dedicated community can be.

23

I preached a three-weekend parish retreat for the people of St. Gabriel parish and marveled at their enthusiastic response. I attended the funeral of Father Jack Schindler, who died suddenly, and I realized once again that it could be over for me at any time as well. I designed a plate at Louisville Stoneware for a charity auction to feed the hungry. It reminded me once again how lucky we are compared to most of the world.

I celebrated Christmas with my family in Meade County and realized once again how important my family is to me and how much I love them. I attended the ordination of two of our seminarians to the diaconate and was reminded once again of the courage of our young priests-to-be.

I was honored to preach the Bellarmine University Baccalaureate Mass for the eighth time. There are some great young adults out there. With mixed feelings, I said good-bye to my job as a vocation director, to which I gave all the enthusiasm I could muster. What a month! I even got a Christmas card from two of my old grade-school girl friends. Yes, two!

As we end the Christmas season once more, I have been reminded again that God comes to us especially in the very ordinary, not the spectacular and dramatic, events of life. That, I believe, was the message of Christmas. Like Jeremiah, I found God this last year, not in the blowing wind or the roaring fire but in the quiet whispering breeze of ordinary people's lives.

January 8, 2004

A Story of God's Unbelievable Generosity

Each one of them received a full day's pay. Matthew 20

The parable of the "vineyard workers" is enough to make wine growers all over the world cringe. This parable is not an instruction on how to operate a successful vineyard. If you followed this example, you would be broke in no time. It's a story about how God treats us, a story about God's unbelievable generosity.

The whole purpose of this parable is to shock in order to instruct. This parable is insane, according to human thinking, but that's the point of the parable. That's its genius. It tells of God's unexpected, insane love for us, no matter what we have done or what we have failed to do! That's why it is called the Gospel, "the good news."

Those who had "worked all day in the sun" were the religious authorities. Those "hour-before-quitting-time" workers were the tax collectors and sinners, those who felt unworthy in God's eyes, simple people who followed Jesus.

You can imagine how both groups reacted when they heard the punch line, "Give them all a full day's pay." It's very close to the message of another parable: the father who loves both his sons, the one who stayed as well as the one who strayed. The message is simple: God loves all his children, no matter what they have done or failed to do for God.

The tax collectors, sinners and rejects were delirious with joy when they heard that message. The Scribes and Pharisees, who taught that God's love depended on people's behaviors, were outraged. In the words of Jesus, they were "envious because I am generous."

They made the mistake of believing that there is not enough love to go around.

One of the worst things to happen to the church occurred when it started to "conditionalize" the "good news." It said, "God will love you if you do this, and God won't love you if you do that." It is not uncommon to hear some religious people tone down the "good news" because it is too dangerous.

Their worst nightmare is that if people really believed the message of this parable and the church really taught it, all hell would break loose. People would do anything they want. That's what worried the Scribes and Pharisees. In reality the opposite was true in Jesus' day, as it is in ours.

What do you believe? Are you one of those people who still believes that God pays us with love depending how many hours we have loved him? Are you one of those people who still believes that God turns his love on and off, depending what we do or fail to do?

If you are, really listen to the message of this parable. If it sounds too good to be true, then you got the message. God's incredible unconditional love does sound too good to be true, but the fact of the matter is, it is true.

January 15, 2004

26

Sometimes We All Have Too Much Baggage

Take nothing for the journey. Stay at whatever house you enter. When people will not receive you, leave that town, shaking its dust from your feet. Luke 9

Every year in January, I have the practice of going through my house and getting rid of stuff. Though people have called my house "minimal," I still have too much baggage.

Sometimes my stuff owns me. It has to be cleaned around, boxed, stacked, stored, filed and even insured. I especially hate it when I have to go digging for something at the bottom of all that stuff. I know people who never get rid of anything.

Likewise, we seem to hang onto old memories, hurts, fears, dreads, ideas and regrets even when they drag us down and make us sick. Sometimes these anxieties own us. They are rehearsed, gone over, obsessed about and discussed until they drive us and those around us a little crazy. January is also a good month to clean out our hearts as well as our closets.

Not all of us are first-century missionaries, but the advice Jesus gave his disciples back then can help us 21st-century Christians. Travel light. Be happy with what you have. Let go.

We live in a culture obsessed with material things, with having and owning. Sometimes the having is a prison in itself. The more we have, the more we have to maintain and protect. Fear of losing it all often drains us of time and energy and fills us with anxiety.

"Happy are the poor in spirit." Happy are those who are free from craving, free from the work of keeping, free of the anxiety that comes from the fear of losing what we have and free of the distance that too many things creates between ourselves and others.

Living is one thing, and getting ready to live is another. One of the saddest TV shows I've ever seen was one about the widows of Florida whose husbands worked themselves into an early grave so that they could "really live" some magic day in the future.

Many of us live in a world of never enough: never enough money, never enough friends and never enough time. Unable to appreciate what we have, we put off being happy until some imagined time, person or windfall comes into our lives. *Carpe diem* — seize the day. We have enough to be happy right now, even in the face of problems, if we care to.

So much of our baggage is invisible from the outside. Sometimes the heaviest baggage of all is mental: worry, regret and dread. When we hold onto those things, we fail to seize the day. We live in the past or a day that has not yet arrived.

The source of all that baggage is the inability to let go and trust in God's providence, the inability to do one's best and let go of what did happen or what might happen. That's what Jesus meant by "my peace I leave with you."

January 22, 2004

Preparing Young Couples for Marriage

Take care lest any of you fall away from the living God. Encourage one another. We have become partners with Christ if only we maintain to the end that confidence with which we began. Hebrews 3:12-14

When I am called on to prepare young couples for marriage, I like to encourage them to look around, not for some television idol but for the oldest couple they know who are still in their first marriage and who still have a twinkle in their eyes for each other. When they find such a couple, I encourage them to have a good heart-to-heart talk with them.

One of those couples used to walk past my house when the weather was nice. They were so cute, shuffling hand-in-hand and leaning on each other like canes. Though they were old, their body language screamed "love" as they looked lovingly at each other and chatted about God-knows-what.

When I would see them, I would try to imagine how many trials and tribulations they had survived in their 60, maybe 70 or more years of marriage. I am sure they had hundreds of reasons to give up on their marriage, but they didn't. To me, they were walking parables of fidelity in a world littered with infidelities.

They are not only an inspiration to young couples, they also are an inspiration to priests such as me. We, too, have made our commitment versions of "for better, for worse; for richer, for poorer; in sickness, in health, until death."

We are priests forever. Ordination is not magic, nor is marriage. On many days the grass looks greener on the other side of the fence for us, too. Sometimes there seem to be better reasons to quit than go on.

The Letter to the Hebrews talks a lot about perseverance and fidelity. In spite of the weakness of individuals within the faith community and persecution from outside the community, the writer encourages individual Christians to remain faithful. In simple phrases, the writer outlines how to remain faithful: "keep your eyes fixed on Jesus," "take care," "encourage one another" and "maintain that confidence with which we began."

This column is about encouraging Catholics to remain faithful to our church. As you know, many of our fellow Catholics have left for "greener pastures." For those who stay, the reasons to give up sometimes seem more convincing than the reasons to stay.

I find the words of the Letter to the Hebrews just as comforting today as they must have been to their original readers. Personally, I have been able to remain faithful to priesthood by keeping my eyes fixed on Jesus, by taking care of my call, by the encouragement I get from good Catholics around this diocese and by remembering the enthusiasm I had when I was first ordained.

I encourage couples, young and old, to do the same. Keep your eyes fixed on Jesus, feed your marriage, encourage each other and remember the enthusiasm of your wedding day.

January 29, 2004

Lord Knows the Church Isn't Perfect

The community of believers were of one heart and one mind. Great respect was paid to them all. Acts of the Apostles 4:32,33

A few years back I was anonymously sipping coffee at McDonald's in the Highlands. Next to me, two old men were gossiping about this and that when the question of Mass attendance came up.

One of the old men snapped back to the other's question, "Naaah! I don't go. They're a bunch of crazies down there, and the priest is as crazy as the rest of them."

I was sitting there nervously biting my nails, waiting to overhear which parish and what priest were being raked over the coals, ready to wing the old geezer with my ham biscuit if they were talking about the Cathedral parish and me, its pastor. I don't know if they smelled a rat or not, but they dropped the subject and moved on to politics.

I was a little disappointed, because I have always secretly wanted to start a fight in a public place and win. Being nice all the time has a way of backing up on a person sometime. I almost had my chance, and it slipped right through my hands.

Though this Scripture passage is about the church on one of its best days, it has never been all sweetness and light. This passage presents us with an extremely idealized snapshot of the early church, but there are many more passages that are not so glamorous.

As Paul Harvey says, "And now for the rest of the story." The reading says members of this idealized community "sold property and donated the proceeds." A few chapters after this rosy passage, we read about Ananias and Sapphira, who donated some of their property to the church, but held back part of the proceeds. When they were confronted about it, they lied and were struck dead. Beware, all of you who have not honored your CSA pledges.

It also says that "they were of one mind and one heart." However, the great missionary team of Paul and Timothy couldn't get along and had to separate, each going his own way. Parish staffs take heart!

It also says "they devoted themselves to the breaking of bread and the prayers and a reverent fear overtook them all." Yet Paul had to write a scathing letter to the new Christians in Corinth. They were showing up for the Eucharist drunk, turning it into a fashion show and discriminating against the poor in their seating arrangements.

Those who drop out and use the flimsy excuse that the church isn't as perfect as it should be, or used to be, merely expose their ignorance of both Scripture and history. The fact of the matter is, God has deliberately chosen idiots, thieves, agnostics, adulterers, liars, weaklings and the handicapped as building blocks for his church.

Besides, if God had expected the church to be perfect, you and I would never have been invited to be part of it.

February 5, 2004

Being Good and Being Righteous

One son said he wouldn't go into the vineyard and work, but did. The other son said he would go, but didn't. Matthew 21:28-30

When I started writing this column, I was more than a little apprehensive about how people would respond. I had to ignore that little voice in my head that always tells me that I am not good enough or smart enough to do such a thing. I also know that "the nail that sticks out is the first to be hammered." Thankfully, the response has been much more positive than I imagined.

I am especially surprised to hear so much positive feedback from non-practicing Catholics. I consider it quite an honor to be able to touch these people with this column. As a popular spiritual writer puts it, "If a teacher is not smart enough and in touch enough with the non-elite peoples to communicate his or her knowledge to them, then that person is in the wrong vocation."

I have always had a soft spot in my heart for the marginalized of our church. I have spent much of my priesthood reaching out to them, and, whenever possible, inviting them to begin again.

I suppose my soft spot comes from my belief that sometimes there is only a hair's difference between belief and non-belief and my observation that church attendance is not always an indicator of faith. I have known some very mean church people, and I have also known some very loving and generous non-practicing church members.

I have come to believe that most non-practicing Catholics yearn for a connection to their church, in spite of the fact that they have sometimes had such empty experiences as church members. I am convinced that they leave more from boredom and disappointment than from loss of faith.

The parable in this reading reminds us that you cannot judge a book by its cover, and you cannot judge people from external signs. It reminds us that God often gets a better hearing and response from the very people whom the righteous and church-going despise.

These are the people who make no claims of being righteous or religious, but who carry on the daily tasks given to them by God. People respond best to God's call when they do not try to be religious, but simply do the will of God through the normal course of living.

The message of this parable is simple. Sometimes God's work gets done beyond the bounds of church activity. Like the older son in another parable, the news that God can have a special love for prodigals often elicits anger in the hearts of those who pride themselves on toeing the line of observance.

I have always taken great comfort in the words of the second Eucharistic Prayer for Reconciliation: "When we were lost and could not find our way to you, you loved us more than ever." It is the awareness of that love, not shaming them, that often brings them back.

February 12, 2004

Celebrating the Sacrament of Marriage

Let marriage be held in honor. Hebrews 13:4

There is a war going on between the popular culture and our church over the celebration of marriage. The war is over the continuous "Hollywood-ization" of the sacrament of marriage, and the church is losing this war. According to "Dear Abby," there are many priests, ministers and rabbis who dread doing weddings for this very reason.

You have all heard the horror stories about rigid priests and inflexible rules. As one young person told me not too long ago, "Father, why is it such a hassle to get married in the Catholic church? You ask too many questions and have too many hoops to jump through. All I want is a wedding in a church."

Some of this is probably true, but there is another set of horror stories that you may not have heard. Every priest has his own horror stories, and here are some of mine.

I have been asked not to have Bible readings. I have been asked if a pop song, with a verse that begins with "The first time I ever lay with you," could be used at Communion.

I ended up in a wedding for a bride who had morning sickness so bad and a groom who was so drunk that they both had to sit down before the wedding was over. At another wedding, some of the guests were actually serving drinks in the back pew during Mass.

I have been tricked into celebrating marriages for people who have no parish, no pastor and no desire to have one. I have been manipulated by couples who sign up as parishioners long enough to get a free wedding, never to be seen or heard from again.

I have suffered through marriage preparation where the only concerns have been dresses, cakes, flowers and photographs. I have been verbally abused by people who met each other only two months before and refused to go through the mandatory six-month preparation (erroneously referred to as a six-month wait).

And, yes, I have had many, many wonderful weddings for cooperative people with their priorities straight — people who are serious about their religion and who understand that the church is not trying to hassle them, but to preserve the sacred institution of marriage from constant compromise.

People tend to mimic weddings they have seen. Weddings in the church should set an example for the younger couples to follow. A good wedding is a wonderful opportunity to teach new couples and re-inspire older couples about what's truly important.

I would like to remind all the young couples who are contemplating marriage this spring that, in our church, we don't just "do weddings"; we "celebrate the Sacrament of Marriage." That's what distinguishes priests and deacons from judges, ministers and justices of the peace. Since we teach the permanence of marriage, we must work together to prepare carefully and well, not just for a wedding but also for a marriage.

February 19, 2004

Our God Wants to Give Us Good Things

Devote yourselves to prayer. Colossians 4:2

On Ash Wednesday, we committed ourselves once again to the traditional spiritual disciplines of prayer, fasting and almsgiving. In this column, I would like to review some basic teachings from Jesus on prayer.

The first thing we need to know about prayer is the kind of God to whom we pray. Jesus taught us to address God as "abba!" Jesus raised more than a few eyebrows when he addressed God with this word. Remember that the Jews at one point in their history considered God's name to be so holy that it could not be spoken. Here Jesus tells us to call God "abba!"

"Abba" and "imma" (mama and daddy in Hebrew) were the ways little children at that time would address their hugging and affectionate parents. Jesus did not use those formal titles to represent a strict and disciplined home where kids are scared of their parents. No, Jesus, wanted us to know we have a God who dotes on us and wants us to have everything we need.

Jesus also told us that we don't have to "rattle on like the pagans who believe they can wear God down to get what they want by the sheer multiplication of words." What does it mean to "pray like a pagan?"

Pagans are scared of their gods. Their gods are moody. Their gods have to be bribed, pleaded with and begged. The whole idea of pagan prayer is to get their gods to change their minds by buttering them up. Christians don't have to butter up their God to get good things. Our God already wants to give us good things.

Finally, Jesus tells us that God will give us those things that are good for us, at the time they are good for us, and not just those things that look good to us. He uses three examples: a stone that only looks like a scone; a poisonous eel that looks like a fish; and a rolled up scorpion that looks like a speckled egg.

Yes, God gives us what is good for us, but will not give us those things that simply look good to us, any more than a good parent would give a child a bottle of Drano simply because he cries for it.

As we move through this holy season of Lent, we can do nothing better than recommit to a more intense effort at both communal prayer and private prayer.

Even if we cannot go to church more than once a week to pray with our faith community, we can commit to a more focused approach when we do go. Even in an active life, we can be creative in finding moments here and there for private prayer: on a walk, in the car or by rising a few minutes before everyone else. As Henry Ford would say, "Those who think they can and those who think they can't are both right."

February 26, 2004

We are "Like Nurslings Carried in God's Arms"

Like a weaned child on its mother's lap,
so is my soul within me. Psalm 131:2

An old rocking chair recently came into my possession. I was told it belonged to my family years ago, but my mother had given it to one of my aunts somewhere along the way.

I certainly remember a rocking chair from my childhood days, but I was skeptical that it was the same one until I saw it. It has some deep cut marks on one of the arms. As soon as I saw it, I remembered being punished as a young boy for laying a board across that rocker and sawing through it, into one of the arms of that chair.

It was in that chair that I also had one of my earliest and clearest childhood memories. I don't know how old I was — maybe four — but I remember being rocked to sleep in that chair by my mother one spring afternoon. I can even remember those old-fashioned sheer curtains, blowing in the breeze of the open window in front of us. I still remember feeling so special, so loved, so filled with peace at that moment, nestled in my mother's arms.

Pope John Paul I, who lived for only a month after he became pope, once said that God is both male and female, but more female than male. Scripture has many references to the feminine qualities of God. Jesus, lamenting the cold reception he was getting from the religious authorities, once said, "How often have I wanted to hug you to me, like a mother hen brings her chicks under her wings, but you would not have it!"

Isaiah says that we are "like nurslings, carried in God's arms and fondled in his lap," and "as a mother comforts her son, God will comfort us." Every parish hymnal in this country has the hymn, built on another text from Isaiah, "Like a shepherd he feeds his flock and gathers the lambs in his arms, holding them close to his heart."

People who have heard me preach over the years are familiar with a life-changing dream I had as a young priest. I have talked about it many times.

In that dream, I was sitting in a folding lawn chair on a treeless, grassy mound-of-a-mountain watching the sun go down. Even though I knew that God was sitting beside me in another folding chair, I could not look over.

We simply sat there peacefully, in silence, watching the sun. We were both smoking cheap King Edward cigars. Finally, God leaned over and whispered in my ear, "Ron, isn't this wonderful?"

With that I woke up. My relationship with God took a dramatic turn that day, after that dream. Instead of being the scolding male figure I grew up with, my experience of God in the last 30 years has been more like that spring afternoon, many years ago, when I was rocked to sleep by my mother.

March 4, 2004

"The Truth Lies in the Middle"

The servant of the Lord must not be quarrelsome but must be kindly toward all. He must be an apt teacher, patiently and gently correcting those who contradict him, in hope always that God will enable them to repent and know the truth. 2 Timothy 2:24-25

Cornelius and Cyprian may not be names that people give their kids these days, but make no mistake about it, these two guys are ancient heroes in the church's growing list of canonized saints. The church celebrates these two saints together for a reason.

Cornelius and Cyprian were friends and fellow bishops from the third century. The third century was a difficult time in the church, so dangerous that these two bishops and many others like them ended up as martyrs. Cornelius and Cyprian were separated by distance, but they dealt with the same issues and encouraged each other.

Cornelius was a Roman who was elected pope 12 months after the martyrdom of Pope Fabian. Cyprian, a rich, pagan teacher and lawyer from north Africa, became a Christian and very soon a bishop. Pope Cornelius died from hardships caused by exile. Bishop Cyprian's head was cut off.

During those very difficult times in the church, many Christians abandoned the faith out of fear of being killed. When some of them sought to return to the church in better times, some bishops welcomed them back as if nothing had happened. Others would not allow any of them to return at all.

41

Cornelius said that people who gave up their faith should be welcomed back, but only after doing penance. This was a wise middle course between the two extremes. Cyprian supported Cornelius in this position.

In Paul's letters to Timothy, he outlines for his young fellow missionary the qualities a bishop should have. A bishop, he wrote, should be irreproachable, even-tempered, self-controlled, modest and hospitable — all the things the Pope Cornelius and Bishop Cyprian exemplified.

In a church being split apart today by fanatics at both ends of the spectrum, Sts. Cornelius and Cyprian have a lot to teach us. The best bishops, pastors and church members today, like always, are those who ignore zealots of every stripe and listen to the less shrill voices of reason and joy. Zealotry always fails, because it makes people think they can demonstrate their commitment by forcing their point of view onto others.

"Virtus stat in medio" — "the truth lies in the middle." This is the difference between knowledge and wisdom. We don't need just smart leaders. We need wise leaders. Especially today, we need people who can bring opposing sides together, as Cornelius and Cyprian did way back in the third century.

They ignored fanatics at both ends of the spectrum, and so should we. Fanatics always overstate their case. As I read somewhere several years back, heresy is always the truth exaggerated to the point of distortion.

March 11, 2004

St. Joseph was a Model of Simple Faith

Joseph did as the angel directed him.
Matthew 1

When I first arrived as pastor of the Cathedral of the Assumption, I was regularly attacked by people concerning the statues of Mary and Joseph in the sanctuary. They were created by Bob Lockhart of Bellarmine University and had been placed there during the 1970s renovation.

I liked them, but many did not. They irritated the traditional sensitivities of many pious Catholics.

Mary and Joseph were portrayed in very realistic, first-century Palestinian clothes. Mary was old and weather-worn, as she would have looked at the end of her life at the time of her assumption into heaven. Joseph stood there slumped, like a tired worker, with his mouth open in awe. They are fine pieces of art, and I still believe they would have been more accepted if they had been displayed in a better fashion.

Tomorrow is the feast of St. Joseph. Ever since my Cathedral days, on this feast I especially think about Bob Lockhart's sculptures. I believe he did a good job portraying Joseph by having him standing there with his mouth open. What better way to picture this well-known, but little-known-about, saint. Standing in awe, with mouth open, captures the fidelity, simplicity and openness of this holy man.

I remember one of my theology professors saying that holiness sometimes comes down to "shutting up and putting up." Nobody embodies that idea more than this quiet and faithful servant of God, husband of Mary and foster father to the boy Jesus.

In the last several years, I cannot think of St. Joseph without thinking of our beloved Bishop Maloney. He is a quiet man of faith who has served the church in good times and in bad, through thick and thin. "Always a bridesmaid and never a bride," he has always served quietly by making others look good. Like the moon, he has always reflected the light of others. And Like St. Joseph, he "shut up and put up."

In a world that overvalues the rational thinking of the human mind, St. Joseph stands, with his mouth open in awe, as a model of simple faith. He did not always understand what was going on with God, but he accepted God's will in his life with perfect trust and unquestioning faith.

The faith of simple people is, more often than not, the best faith. Did not Jesus once pray, "Father, Lord of heaven and earth, to you I offer praise; for what you have hidden from the learned and the clever you have revealed to the merest children." Again he said, "Whoever does not accept the reign of God like a little child shall not take part in it."

Who among us has not stood dumbfounded like St. Joseph, with our jaw dropped, in the face of something that God has done that we do not understand? The real challenge is to trust God in those moments, praying "Lord, I believe. Help my unbelief."

March 18, 2004

Our True Nature Lies Buried Within Us

God created humankind in his own image,
in the divine image he created them.
Genesis 1:27

There is an old story from another religious tradition that I have always found fascinating, a story about the creation and fall of humankind. According to this tradition, humankind was created in the beginning to be like God, but somehow lost its awareness of divinity by turning away from God.

After this loss, the angels got together to decide where to hide the secret of humankind's divinity so that humans would never find it. One angel suggested that they hide it deep in the earth. This idea was rejected, because the other angels feared that humans might one day tunnel deep into the earth and find it.

A second angel suggested that they place it on some distant star. Again the other angels rejected the idea fearing that someday humans might walk upon the stars and find it.

After considering many ideas, the angels finally decided that they would bury this secret deep within humans themselves because they knew they would never think to look there. And so they buried the secret of our divinity deep within us, and even today we do not know to look there.

As the book of Genesis tells us, every one of us has been created in the image and likeness of God, with godlike qualities and powers within us. However, many of us never realize our true nature, nor act on it. It lies buried within us like some undiscovered treasure.

When we are unaware of our own godlike power, we tend to turn our lives over to others. When we do that, we end up becoming victims of what other people decide for us, all the while complaining of the outcome.

We end up like the rider on a runaway horse in a story I read years ago. A farmer was walking down the road when a man on a bridle-less horse galloped by him. The farmer called out, "Hey, where are you going?" The panicked rider yelled back, "Don't ask me, ask the horse!"

When we are unaware of our own godlike power and turn our lives over to others, we often end up blaming and reviling them for our unhappy conditions. We blame our unhappiness and sad situations on dead parents, old teachers, former spouses and even God himself. This is a simple way of excusing our own laziness when faced with the job of building a life for ourselves.

When we are unaware of our own godlike power, we often fall into the trap of conforming, without question, to the values of the popular culture so that others will approve of us. Slaves of conformity, our life script becomes, "Everybody else is doing it."

As Marianne Williamson writes, "Our deepest fear is not that we are inadequate. Our deepest fear is that we are powerful beyond measure. It is our light, not our darkness, that most frightens us."

March 25, 2004

Paying Attention to What's Important

Your Word is a lamp for my feet, a light for my path. Psalm 119:105

If you want to see human weirdness in action, just go to the grocery store. I thought I had seen it all until, a few years ago, I saw a woman unscrewing salad dressing tops one after another, sticking her finger on the inside of the caps, putting that same finger to her tongue for a taste, frowning and screwing the tops back on before going to the next one.

Not too long ago, I was in a grocery store again. In front of me was a woman pushing a cart with a cell phone at her ear, a child on her hip and another one in a cart. She was reading labels and throwing things in the cart.

The kid in the cart was about to jump ship and the other was crying. Missing the basket, she dropped a carton of eggs, yelled "sit down" into the phone and ran into a pyramid of cheese stacked precariously in the aisle. All of a sudden her whole balancing act came crashing down around her.

When a million things are vying for our attention at the same time, we end up paying real attention to nothing. What voice gives you direction? From what source do you get instructions about how to live your life?

For Christians, our marching orders come from the Word of God. In the Liturgy of the Word, we sit each week at the feet of our master to be taught how we should live. If we are to pattern our lives on Jesus, then we need to know who Jesus was, what he taught, how he lived and what he wants from us.

We Catholics are not known for our knowledge of, and love for, the Word. There is a reason. Stung by the spawning of breakaway churches during the Protestant revolt of the 16th century, a revolt by people who were privately interpreting the Scriptures and coming up with all kids of contradictory teachings, the church, in an attempt to protect the Word from false doctrines, overprotected it to the point of keeping it from the very people for whom it was intended.

At that big, messy divorce, Roman Catholics took the altar and Protestants took the pulpit. A typical Protestant church has a big pulpit and small altar. A typical Catholic church has a large altar and small pulpit.

One of the greatest things to come out of Vatican II was the giving of the Word back to Catholic people: at Mass, in the sacraments, in Bible study groups and in several new modern translations. When it comes to the Word, we Catholics have come a long way in the last 30 years.

The Word proclaimed and preached is a "lamp unto our feet." It guides us on the right path. At Mass, we are invited to "feed on" the Eucharist, but we are also invited to "feed on" the Word.

April 1, 2004

48

A Word of Praise for our Priests

You are a priest forever. Psalm 110:4

Today is Holy Thursday, the day we not only celebrate the memory of the first Eucharist, but also celebrate the call to priestly service in the church. Part of that celebration is dedicated to the renewal of our commitments as priests.

Over the last two years, we as a church have been forced to focus on the priests who have failed. Most of us remaining priests are still grieving the loss of several of our brother priests, doing our best to pick up the slack and struggling to remain faithful ourselves.

Motives are being purified. As Archbishop Quinn wrote: "This is the best time in the history of the church to be a priest, because it is a time when there can only be one reason for being a priest or for remaining a priest — that is, to 'be with' Christ. It is not for perks or applause or respect or position or money or other worldly gain or advantage. These things either no longer exist or are swiftly passing."

It is dangerous to single out a few of our priests from the whole presbyterate, but that will not stop me. Besides, as St. Paul writes, "if one part is honored, all the parts share its joy." Here are just a sampling of the priests I admire, and priests who bring all of us joy.

I have always admired Father Thomas Clark for his ability and willingness to take the difficult assignments, many times in places that no one else will take. I have been proud to be in the same presbyterate with Father Nick Rice. He has made our presbyterate proud by serving in several national organizations, especially as president of the National Federation of Priests' Councils.

Father John Judie is a hero of mine, both for his serious preaching and pastoral abilities and for his interest in the church in Africa. Father Charles Dittmeier, a seminary classmate, also represents our presbyterate in the universal church by serving the deaf in Cambodia.

I can't say enough good things about Father Clyde Crews. He represents those who serve in the academic world. No one has done more than him to gather, protect and teach us about our own history.

No one works harder than Father Joe Graffis, a man of great ability and many talents. Father Dick Sullivan is, in my mind, the quintessential pastor: strong, loving and wise. Father Bill Medley represents to me the balance between seriousness and humor.

Msgr. Joseph O'Bryan and Father Jerry Timmel, our unsung "home missionary" heroes, have my greatest respect. Father Bill Hammer, forever the gentleman, is a man of many talents and great humility. Father Chuck Walker, a good man, always reminds us not to take ourselves too seriously.

On Holy Thursday, remember your priest. Recent research found that resignation from the priesthood, especially among the young, is due to loneliness, feelings of being unappreciated and disillusionment. We can handle anything if we know you are with us.

April 8, 2004

Appreciating the View from the Pew

Stop turning my Father's house into a marketplace. John 2:16

Every priest should have to sit in a pew several times a year for Sunday Mass to experience what lay people experience in an average Catholic parish. There is a world of difference between standing at the altar or pulpit and sitting in a pew. It is a real eye-opener.

During my sabbatical, I often bypassed "concelebrating" in favor of attending church as an anonymous visitor to see and feel what an average Catholic parishioner sees and feels on a typical Sunday morning. I always leave having a lot more compassion for what lay people have to endure in trying to attend Mass. A recent experience in another state was sadly typical.

One of the first things I noticed was the absence of good signs, even in a tourist area. After circling around a few blocks for almost an hour, I finally found the church hidden among some trees. The message I got from this experience was that our church is not very hospitable to visitors or strangers. If I had been ambivalent about going to Mass, this experience alone would have caused me to give up.

Even the church itself did not have a noticeable sign. The first moment I knew for sure it was a Catholic church was when I spotted a big table at the front door selling raffle tickets. If I still had any doubt about what denomination I had stumbled across, it was assuaged by the fact that there were two collections and a "money talk" about the building campaign, thinly disguised as a homily. If I had any doubt left whether the church was "Catholic," it evaporated when the announcement time turned into yet another plug for the building campaign.

I sat near the rear. Throughout the Mass, the new church had a door that banged shut every time another round of late arrivals entered. This continued through the first two readings.

People were talking and shuffling throughout the readings as they do during the previews of a movie, mainly because the sound system was so weak you could barely hear the lectors. Mothers wrestled restless children, doing their best to get something out of what was happening up front while reaching for bottles, rattle toys and little "climbers."

The music was typical "Catholic parish music." It bounced between unsingable, childish and overused. The priest would not shut up. In a grating effort to be "meaningful," he was irritatingly dramatic. He chatted endlessly throughout the Mass, explaining everything from what the readings were to be about to what they meant once they were read, even before the "homily."

Throughout this experience, I remembered a line from a Wynona Judd song, "Heaven Help Me." She sings, "I could lose my religion in my struggle to believe." Somehow, the people were able to focus on the few crumbs of silence and good ritual. My respect and appreciation for what they have to go through rose dramatically that day.

April 15, 2004

Sometimes We All Need
a Second Chance

Sir, give it another year. I will cultivate the ground round it and fertilize it: it may bear fruit in the future. If not, you can cut it down. Luke 13.

This parable is very personal to me. I cannot read it without my mind going back to 1959 and the first semester, second year of high school seminary.

I came to Louisville from Meade County to attend the former St. Thomas Seminary on Old Brownsboro Road. It was a major adjustment for this little 14-year-old country boy. I was a fish out of water.

Instead of offering counseling, the rector of the seminary called me into his office one day. His exact words to me were, "Mr. Knott! We are sending you home in the morning because you are a hopeless case."

With no one to come to my defense, I had to come to my own defense. I cried for another chance, using words very similar to the words of today's parable. "Father, give me another chance. I will try harder. Then, if things aren't better, you can kick me out."

It worked, and here I stand 45 years later, a priest, because of that "second chance." I came very, very close to giving up that day, but by the grace of God I didn't.

In this amazing parable, Jesus teaches his followers that, since the beginning, God has reached out to his people over and over again. Jesus is the culmination of this long history of opportunities.

The God of limitless mercy and compassion is patient with us, hoping that we will "bear fruit" before it is too late, patiently awaiting a response from us until we take our last breath.

Lately, I have never before heard of so many people on the verge of giving up: Catholics on their church, priests on the priesthood, parents on their children, spouses on their marriages and the sick on their treatment. This parable offers a most hopeful message to all of these people.

There is an old story, a favorite of mine, that brings this teaching home. It's about an engineer who designed a tunnel between Switzerland and Austria several years back. He got the idea that the best way to approach the project was to have diggers work from both directions at the same time and meet in the middle.

It was risky, but a much faster method, one that would save lots of time and money. When the day arrived when the diggers were supposed to meet, they didn't. Presuming that he had made a gigantic mistake, he committed suicide. The day of his funeral, the diggers broke through, meeting perfectly. The poor engineer gave up one day too soon.

No matter what others think of you, no matter what you think of yourself, remember this: It ain't over 'til it's over. As long as we are alive, there is hope. With God there are as many second chances as we need.

April 22, 2004

We Should Make Friends with Silence

Jesus went up the mountain to pray. Luke 9

As most of you know, I am on a sabbatical. Sometime last fall, I reached a point where I needed to withdraw so as to find my way again. I spent the whole month of February by myself in a small apartment on the beach in northern Florida. Because of the cool weather at that time of year, there were very few people in the town where I was staying. Often I did not speak to another person for days.

Jesus went up the mountain to pray, to get his bearings, to find out what God wanted him to do next. At the beginning of this Gospel, we are told that Jesus went to the desert for 40 days to get his bearings, to find out what God wanted him to do with his life.

In this text, Jesus is getting close to the end. He goes up a mountain to get his bearings once again. While at prayer, Jesus had a vision of how things were coming together. Strengthened by this insight, Jesus came down the mountain with resolve to go to Jerusalem to embrace his suffering, death and resurrection.

I went to the beach to pray, to get my bearings, to find out what God wants me to do next.

As I listened, I realized that I am facing a decision. On one hand I could take the easy road. I could choose to coast the rest of the way to retirement. I am very aware that this option is open to me, but a voice in my heart of hearts said "no." It said to me, "You are to do the hard thing, the thing that will require more of you, that struggle that will make you keep growing."

If I could recommend anything as a spiritual practice, it would be to make friends with silence. Silence makes you face yourself, challenges you constantly and calls you back to the truth. It is so easy to lose yourself in a world as noisy as ours. If you are facing a major decision and you don't know what to do, go off by yourself in silence.

You don't have to go to a monastery or any other "holy place" to get this clarification. Some people can do this on a camping trip by themselves, with a night or two in a remote cabin on a lake or on a long walk. I suppose if you're from the country, you can do this sitting in a deer stand for days or driving a tractor for long hours. Some can do it while driving back and forth to work.

The possibilities are endless, if you really want it. All you have to do is to embrace this silence rather than try to run from it. If you need clarification about the direction of your life, the best place to get that clarification may just be in the quiet.

April 29, 2004

Thoughts on the Status of the Priesthood

You can tell a tree by its fruit. Matthew 7:20

Father Andrew Greeley, a priest-sociologist, had an interesting article about priests in *The New York Times* recently. He reflected on the negative image of priests in today's scandal-ridden climate. Never shy about pointing out our weaknesses, in this article he put a lot of things in perspective.

Here are a few of the positive things he noted about priests from recent research, especially research done by *The Los Angeles Times* and the National Opinion Research Center at the University of Chicago.

Ninety-six percent of priests are not abusers. A vast majority of priests said that life in the priesthood is better than they expected. Ninety-three percent of all priests said they would choose priesthood again. Priests are more likely to say they are happy and satisfied than are doctors, lawyers, teachers and even Protestant clergy. Priests, on average, seem to be about the happiest men in the country.

Priests compare favorably with married men of similar backgrounds. There is no evidence that priests are more likely to be frustrated, unhappy misfits than are married men.

If this is true, then where does this negative picture of priests come from? One important reason is that the 96 percent of priests who are not abusers tend to be silent when their vocation is attacked — either by men who have left the priesthood or by the public — over the crimes of abusers.

Priests may not want to hear it, but Father Greeley makes a convincing case that the biggest problem with priests is not celibacy or sexual frustration, as the media likes to conclude, but "constraints on excellence in an envy-ridden, rigid and mediocre clerical culture that does a poor job in serving church members."

His solution for improving our image is for us to focus our efforts on upgrading the quality of our work, especially in the area of preaching.

These are hard times for priests. Because of the behavior of a few, we are all under attack. More people are making more demands on fewer priests. Yet in parishes where the pastor is reasonably open, reasonably capable and reasonably secure, the lay response is enthusiastic commitment and dedication, even in this climate.

Another priest who writes honestly about priesthood today, Father Donald Cousens, seems to agree with Father Greeley. He writes, "More than a few veteran observers of the church insist that the most pressing issue facing Catholicism today is the quality of its priestly ministry."

I could not agree more. In fact, I recently published a small book on the subject entitled *Intentional Presbyterates*. Written for priests and seminarians, it is my effort to make a case for getting our act together in order to offer better service, regardless of celibacy or who our next bishop or pope will be. It has attracted great interest, at least in other dioceses.

If we priests don't get our act together soon, we have no hope of attracting new priests, and we will wake up someday in the near future to realize that we have nobody left to lead.

May 6, 2004

An Anniversary Faced with Gratitude

My son, when you come to serve the Lord, prepare yourself for trials. Sirach 2:1

I will celebrate the 34th anniversary of my ordination as a priest this coming Sunday. The only picture I have of my actual ordination is one of me standing in the sacristy a few minutes before we walked into the Cathedral for the ordination. Frowning, with eyes downcast, I look as if I was about to face my own hanging. I wasn't sad; I just knew what I was getting into.

One of the last class assignments I remember from Saint Meinrad was a paper we were required to write on the subject of what we expected from priesthood. If I remember correctly, most wrote one of those pious papers on the ideals of ordained ministry. My paper said that I expected a rough ride, a lot of chaos and a lot of testing. Somebody ridiculed it as "too negative." They are gone. I am still here. I rest my case.

Writing that paper about what we expected from priesthood reminded me of those young couples preparing for marriage of whom I have asked a similar question. "What do you expect out of married life?" Of all the times I have asked that question, I always get the same answers, things like "sharing," "loving," "support" and "happiness."

Not one told me they expected to have problems. Instead of expecting to have rough times and even monumental problems, some conclude that when they do, they have somehow made a tragic mistake, picked the wrong person and need to try it again. Only an idiot would expect a rose garden, be it in marriage or priesthood.

After 34 years of priesthood, I can say that I am still here by the grace of God and "with a little help from my friends." Even in the toughest of times, I have never doubted that I have a vocation to priesthood, nor I have ever doubted that God has been with me. On my 34th anniversary, I am filled with gratitude, not only to God but also to the many faith-filled Catholics I have met along the way.

I thank the monks of Saint Meinrad for teaching me to be flexible. I thank the people of St. Mildred in Somerset for being patient with many of my "young priest ideas." I thank the people of St. Peter Church in Monticello and Good Shepherd Chapel in Whitley City for teaching me how to be imaginative, the people of Holy Name of Mary in Calvary for teaching me how to accept love, the people of the Cathedral of the Assumption for letting me know about the transforming power of preaching and that almost anything is possible.

Would I do it again? I don't answer as quickly as I used to, but the answer is still a firm "yes." With only 10 years to retirement, I want to believe that the best is yet to come.

May 13, 2004

Conservative or Liberal, What's the Point?

Do not conform yourselves to this age, but be transformed by the renewal of your mind, so that you may judge what is God's will, what is good, pleasing and perfect.
Romans 12:2

The last time I attended a circus I was a small child. I remember people swinging from trapezes and knife throwers, but what I remember most was a clown. I can still remember him pulling a banana from his large pockets and peeling it ever so ceremoniously. When he finished, he threw the banana away and ate the peel. Everybody, especially the kids, howled with laughter.

What made it funny, I suppose, is that it reminded us of human nature. We often focus on the non-essential, while neglecting what is essential. What parent has not had a child who, after getting a very expensive toy for Christmas, leaves the toy unattended while playing with the box?

"Liberals" and "conservatives" are both doing it right now in the church. Both seem to be obsessed with focusing on the structure of the church, rather than on its mission. "Liberals" want to change everything, while "conservatives" want to change nothing. In the meantime, focusing on "conversion of heart" goes unattended.

"Liberals" believe in "reformation." "Conservatives" believe in "preservation." What Jesus focused on was "transformation."

In the desert, Jesus rejected the devil's temptations to change "things." Jesus left the desert with the determination that what needed changing was people's hearts. The Greek word for what Jesus wanted from us is "metanoia," a radical interior change of thinking that leads to a new way of acting.

If we are not converted in our hearts, we will always end up blindly destroying our sacred structures in our arrogance or blindly preserving them in our rigidity when they need to go. If we are not converted in our hearts, we will always be locked in a vicious war over who really loves the church.

Kenneth Woodward wrote something in *Commonweal* in 1994 that has always made sense to me, something I could have written myself. He said: "I have done my share of institutional criticism, but what offends me is the romantic notion that all the ills of the church reside within the institution — so that if only we could reform it, we ourselves would be better Christians. The truth quite often is the other way around."

In recent Catholicism, the call for inner conversion is being drowned out by the calls to reform or preserve our traditional structures. Who cares who is pope or bishop, what language we use in liturgy, whether we stand or kneel, if we are not living the life of Jesus?

The way out of all the infighting, bickering and name-calling going on in our church is not to make winners and losers out of each other in our structural wars, but to focus on hearing and putting into practice all that Jesus taught us. Christianity was an inner path long before it became a world religion.

May 20, 2004

62

The Human Way, or the "Chicken" Way?

We honor the members we consider less honorable by clothing them with greater care, thus bestowing on the less presentable a propriety which the more presentable already have. 1 Corinthians 12:23, 24

I am somewhat familiar with chickens. We raised them when I was a child.

They, like humans, have patterns of behavior. Chickens are, for the most part, harmless. Their lives seem to revolve solely around food and reproduction. They do have, however, one disturbing trait that bothered me, even as a child. Weak or sick chickens were often pecked at by other chickens until they died from the exhaustion of trying to defend themselves. It must be some evolutionary survival thing that has to do with the availability of food. "The fewer of us, the more for me."

Many kids have their own version of this trait. It's called "bullying": name-calling, physical abuse, humiliation and teasing. I believe that many adults seriously underestimate the damage this does to some kids. This constant pecking away kills the soul, even if it doesn't always kill the body.

Sometimes it even kills the body. Matthew Shephard, a young gay man from Colorado, was tied to a fence post, beaten and left to die in freezing weather. More than half of all male teen suicides are related to sexual orientation issues.

Gossip is not harmless entertainment. When enough people repeat a lie, serious lifelong damage can result. Even passing along an awful truth can destroy another's hope of recovery. "Sticks and stones may break my bones, but words will never hurt me"? Wrong!

Church people may be the worst culprits of all in identifying, labeling, condemning and isolating religious non-conformists. Instead of searching out the lost for healing and special care, they are identified for shunning and judgment by the self-righteous — in the name of God, of course.

Racism, sexism and ageism are all versions of this awful trait. Anytime we set up this "them and us" thinking, subtle and not-so-subtle discrimination and even persecution often follow, especially if these target people are weak and vulnerable.

I suppose one reason for all this comes from a basic fear of shortage: fear of a shortage of love, resources or attention. "Fewer of us means more for me."

Another reason may be that putting others down is an easy shortcut to feeling good about ourselves. "For me to win, you need to lose." Many people, in their effort to prove something about themselves, go looking for enemies. They always find them.

Pecking at the weak may be the "chicken way" to do things. The "Christian way" is different. The Christian way is clearly outlined by St. Paul in his second letter to the church at Corinth. Christians look for ways of pulling people up, rather than putting them down. Christians look for ways to include, rather than exclude. Christians look for ways to "clothe the less honorable with greater care," "giving the less presentable the same propriety as the more presentable."

May 27, 2004

God has Given Parents a "Special Grace"

They even brought babies to be touched by him. When the disciples saw this, they scolded them roundly; but Jesus called for the children, saying: "Let the little children come to me. Do not shut them off. The reign of God belongs to such as these."
Luke 18:15-16

If I were St. Peter guarding the gates of heaven, I would wave anyone through who ever tried to raise children, no questions asked. As a mere observer of those who have the courage to parent, it appears to me to be the most difficult of all callings.

I like to go to the beach for vacations. Every year I usually limp onto the plane, exhausted, with my one suitcase in hand, looking forward to some time by myself. Lately, I have become riddled with guilt as I witness young parents headed to the same beach wrestling crying kids and lugging a truckload of strollers, toys and suitcases.

While I have the luxury of going on vacation, I am aware that many young families neither have the time nor the money for such extravagances. Those lucky few who have managed to save up enough extra money seem to have more patience than Job. God must give them some kind of special grace. If I had to do that, I would probably have to admit myself to a hospital when I got home.

Yes, God must give them some kind of very special grace, such as how to tell the difference between a squeal of delight and a squeal of pain. While I get to decide where and what I want to eat, when I want to get up and go to bed, when I want to go out on the beach and when to come in, young parents don't. They are continuously at the mercy of their kids.

While I can sit in a chair, read a book or even doze off, these parents have to continuously stand guard. They have to watch the water, kiss "boo-boos," referee fights, be constantly on the lookout for strangers who show too much interest in their kids and, worst of all, build sandcastles for hours on end.

On vacation, I go to bed when I am tired. They go to bed only after their children have quit digging their heels in over taking a bath, brushing their teeth or whether they can keep watching TV for another hour.

I can sleep as late as I want and enjoy a leisurely breakfast at some nice restaurant. They have to get up when the kids wake up, usually at the crack of dawn, no matter how tired they are. Once up, the kids have to be dressed and fed before they pack another set of bags for another endless day of castle-building on the beach.

A word to my brother priests: think twice the next time you whine about the celibacy law. The silver lining in that cloud may be bigger than you think.

June 3, 2004

Sometimes We Need to Accept Forgiveness

Peter was distressed that Jesus had said to him a third time, "Do you love me?" And Peter said to him, "Lord, you know everything; you know that I love you." John 21:17

St. Peter is a hero of mine. His real name, of course, was Simon. "Peter" (from the Latin word "petros") was just a nickname meaning "a rock." Today, we might call him "Rocky."

Jesus must have given him that name tongue-in-cheek, because Simon was anything but rock-solid. I am sure the other apostles laughed their heads off when they heard Jesus give him that name.

The story in today's reading takes place during those depressing and confusing few days after Jesus' death and resurrection. Not knowing what to do with themselves, thinking that their dreams about a wonderful kingdom were over, Peter and some of the others returned to their old jobs of fishing.

Appearing to them on the beach after a big catch, Jesus began to question Peter, giving him a chance to retract his three-time denial. You can just imagine Peter squirming with embarrassment as Jesus teasingly asked him three times whether he loved him.

This story reminds me that it is hard to forgive others when they have disappointed and hurt us. But accepting forgiveness from others and forgiving ourselves when we have hurt and disappointed others is often just as difficult. Peter and Judas have a lot to teach us.

Both Judas and Peter denied Jesus, but there was a great difference. Judas could not forgive himself and committed suicide. Jesus, I am convinced, would have forgiven Judas, but Judas never gave Jesus the chance. Peter, on the other hand, accepted Jesus' forgiveness and came to forgive himself, going down in history as a great saint.

Have you ever done some awful, hurtful thing to someone you love, maybe your parents or your children, a spouse or a close friend? Have you ever done something stupid to hurt yourself, maybe losing your life savings though compulsive gambling, maybe ruining your marriage because of infidelity or maybe killing someone while driving intoxicated?

Burdened with an inability to forgive yourself, maybe your life is stuck in a cycle of self-hatred. Some kill themselves, little by little, with drugs or alcohol. Some relieve the pain of regret by taking their own lives.

Sometimes those who have the most to be forgiven for are those who come to appreciate God's forgiveness and mercy the most. I have spent my 34 years as a priest focusing my preaching on God's unconditional love and mercy to those who have fallen short. I have seen this message transform the lives of those who can accept it. I have seen many miserable failures go on, as Peter did, to become some of the best disciples of all.

My friends, we have all failed as disciples. But the important thing is that we recover like Peter rather than follow Judas, who could neither forgive himself nor accept God's forgiveness.

June 10, 2004

Listening for the Voice that Will Guide Us

Jesus said, "My sheep hear my voice —
and they follow me." John 10:27

God speaks to me every day — not directly, but through people, events and dreams and especially through the reading of Scripture.

The only time I can remember anything like being spoken to by God directly was a few years ago after I left the Cathedral of the Assumption. I was moping around the house in a funk, worried about whether I could ever get interested in anything the way I was interested in the Cathedral. My mind was obsessed with negative mind chatter. I was home alone.

All of a sudden I heard a voice, clear and distinct, that said, "Don't worry." It startled me. I look around thinking that it came from the TV. It wasn't even on. I thought I might have left the front door open and a friend had slipped in unheard. There was no one there. I will never know for sure whether I really heard it or just imagined it, but regardless, it was a very helpful message.

God speaks to me every day, especially through the reading of Scripture. One of the advantages of having to preach so often is that the study of Scripture is built into my job.

This advantage does not make me a better person, but it does carry greater responsibility. As the Letter to James says, "When a person knows the right thing to do and does not do it, he sins." Father Charles Nerinckx, a famous Kentucky frontier priest, once wrote, "He who presides over the keeping of the rules should be the first observer of them." Pope Gregory the Great once said, "No one does more harm to the church than he who, having the title or rank of holiness, acts evilly."

This advantage can also make you cringe. The other day I was watching TV and a young Catholic said to her friend, "As someone famous once said, I forget who, 'Thou shalt not kill.'"

I have seen several self-identified Catholics on game shows who couldn't say whether a very familiar quote came from Shakespeare, the Bible or a Hollywood star.

One of Jesus' very favorite images of himself was as a "good shepherd." In our text today, he focuses on the voice of the shepherd.

The voice of the shepherd was extremely important. Sheep roamed, and fences were few. Flocks often mingled during the day as they searched for the scarce grass among the rocks. When evening came, the time for them to be penned up for the night, all a shepherd had to do was to call out. His sheep culled themselves from all the others simply by being able to distinguish his voice from all the other calling voices filling the air.

The question Jesus asks is rather simple: as you graze through life, whose voice do pick out from the many voices calling out to you? Which of those competing voices do you listen to for guidance and direction?

June 17, 2004

Some Words of Guidance for College Graduates

I have set before you life and death, the blessing and the curse. Choose life, then, that you and your descendants may live, by loving the Lord your God, heeding his voice and holding fast to him. Deuteronomy 30: 19, 20

Do you want what's behind door number one, door number two or door number three? Do you want to keep the new kitchen appliances that you have already won, or would you like to trade them for what's behind the curtain on stage?

Some of you may remember the long-running TV show, "Let's Make a Deal." Sometimes contestants' choices would bring them a Hawaiian vacation package or a new car and sometimes a disappointing booby prize. It was a TV version of a "double or nothing" bet in poker.

The program was popular, I believe, because it was symbolic of the human predicament.

All of us, especially this year's college graduates, are faced with a world of choices. Sometimes our choices produce great blessings, and sometimes they bring disasters to us and those around us.

In our reading, the Israelites are about to enter the "promised land" after an arduous trip across the Sinai desert. Before they start their exciting new lives in the land of plenty, Moses lectures them about the necessity of making good choices in a land filled with both blessings and curses. Their happiness, he tells them, will depend in a great measure on how they choose to choose.

In many ways, our graduates are entering a "promised land, flowing with milk and honey" after having survived the arduous journey of college. And they, too, have choices to make. They need to know that their freedom to choose does not guarantee that they will make good choices. The world they are entering is full of smart people doing a whole lot of dumb things, a world knee-deep in the fallout from people's bad choices.

It is important that they choose wisely, because their choices could bring blessings on them and those around them, or they could bring ruin to them and the rest of us as well.

They need to know that they were not created — and they have not been educated — merely for their own good. As Jesus tells his followers, "No one lights a lamp and puts it under a bushel basket or under a bed; he puts it on a lamp stand so that whoever comes in can see it." Their choices will either be part of the solution or part of the problem.

Graduates, make good choices, and let your light shine. Do it for your own good and the good of the world in which you will live, work and raise your children. And, yes, do it for the world the rest of us will be living in as well. We need you to be both good and good at what you do. God is there to help you, and we are here to support you. Congratulations, good luck and may God's wisdom be with you.

June 24, 2004

Jesus is the Real Teacher about Love

I give you a new commandment: love one
another. As I have loved you, so should
you love one another. John 13

After presiding at weddings for 35 years, I am convinced that
many young couples don't have a very good understanding of what
they are promising to do when they make their wedding vows.

George Bernard Shaw probably described this misunderstand-
ing best when he wrote, "When two people are under the influence
of the most violent, most insane, most delusive and most transient of
passions, they are required to swear that they will remain in that ex-
cited, abnormal and exhausting condition continuously until death
do they part."

What many young couples think the marriage vows mean is pledg-
ing to have strong feelings of attraction for their partner for life. No
wonder more than half of them end up disappointed.

Dr. M. Scott Peck says that what most people mean when they
talk about "love" is really a process called "cathexis" or "having strong
feelings of attraction for another person." It is also called "falling in
love."

Real love has very little to do with "feeling good." It's really about
"being good and doing good for another," whether it feels good or
not. In fact, one should be very suspicious of merely having "strong
feelings of attraction" for another person. You may not be "in love."

People who marry simply because they have "strong feelings of
attraction" for each other may wake up one day and realize that those
feelings have passed or have been transferred to yet another. We

call that "falling out of love." There has to be something solid under all those strong "feelings."

Jesus is the real teacher about love, not Hollywood. Why anybody would listen to Hollywood, to a bunch of people who are multiple-time losers in the love department, is beyond my comprehension. Jesus tells us "to love as he loved us."

How did Jesus love us? "While we were still sinners he died for us." We are loved, not because God gets a lot of respect and appreciation from us, not because God gets anything out of it, not because we have done anything to deserve it, but simply because God chooses to love us, without condition, no ifs, ands or buts about it, no matter what we've done or failed to do.

God's love for us is not the famous 50-50 thing that we always hear about marriage. It is 100 percent regardless of what is given back. That is what real love is all about.

Weddings, like ordinations, are not magic. A loser never makes a good priest, and two losers have never made a happy marriage. If you are going to pledge to love someone "as God has loved you," find out how God loves you and let God be your guiding light, not the soap opera by the same name. The quality of your life for the rest of your life may depend on it.

July 1, 2004

We are all Ambassadors for Christ

To whom much is given, much is expected.
More will be asked of the one to whom
more has been entrusted. Luke 12:48

I have always been intrigued by these words of Jesus. I used to think that they were meant for other people: people who have more money, more talent and more status in the community. It was only later that I realized that they are meant for me, too. As I told someone recently in a discussion about winning the lottery, "We have already won the lottery, compared to most of the world."

We have all been given gifts and talents. The more we have been given, the more responsibility we have to use it wisely, not just for ourselves, but for the benefit of the whole community.

Recently, I presided at the funeral of a wonderfully blessed and talented Catholic woman of our community, Mrs. Katty Smith. Her obituary was impressive. Among her many charitable boards and activities were Maryhurst, Wayside Christian Mission, Frazier Rehabilitation Center, Jewish Hospital Health Care Services, the Center for Women and Families and the Cathedral Heritage Foundation.

The list of her involvements in the arts community and political groups was long. She had even sponsored three Cuban girls through Catholic Charities and two Vietnamese families through St. Leonard parish. She knew she was blessed with resources and talent, and she accepted the responsibility that went with them.

There are many good Catholic men and women in our church, people of means, who are doing God's work in our larger community: people such as Christy Brown, Bert Paradis and Marea Gardner.

They are like the women in Luke's Gospel who traveled with Jesus and his apostles, "assisting them out of their means."

Unfortunately, they are often more recognized by the community at large than by the church because they tend not to be lectors, CCD teachers, youth-group leaders or picnic workers, all of whom are needed to carry on the work of the church.

We are all ambassadors for Christ. All of us are called to carry on some part of Christ's work. We can only do that when we are able to recognize our own gifts and talents, and then recognizing them, put them at the service of our brothers and sisters.

All of us have something to share and something to give. Those who have little to give are required to share what they have. Those who have been given more are required to share more. No one is off the hook.

As I reminded the family and friends gathered at Mrs. Smith's funeral, she did not do what she did to earn her way to heaven. She did what she did as an expression of gratitude for all the blessings she had been given. In that she was as generous as God has been to her. That's what "stewardship" is all about: sharing with each other what God has given us, be it our time, our talent or our treasure.

July 8, 2004

Even Judas was Invited to the Last Supper

They all ate and were satisfied. Luke 9

The old "bag lady" entered the church. She was weighted down with shopping bags that held her worldly possessions. Even though it was August, she was dressed in several layers of clothes, all topped off with a ratty old fur. She had the smell of sweaty shoes. As she made her way to the front, people parted to clear the way.

When it came time for Communion, she was in deepest prayer. The ushers came forward to escort people into the Communion line, but they passed over her. Distraught, she turned this way and that, trying to figure out what was happening.

As person after person passed by, she shrugged and began to dig through her bags. Soon she pulled out a loaf of bread, took out a slice and held it lovingly until she heard the priest say, "Body of Christ." With eyes closed, she ate it slowly, knelt down and fell back into deep prayer.

I was reminded of this old tale as I read the story of the feeding of the 5,000. Whenever we see Jesus in an eating event, there are hints of a hidden lesson behind that event. Frequently there is a specific inclusion of society's marginal characters, especially in Luke's Gospel.

This story is preceded by the healing of those in the same crowd who were sick, a marginal class. In the parable of the wedding feast, the good and the bad alike are rounded up and invited to attend. The story of Jesus' meal in the home of Martha and Mary and the Good Samaritan are a set. By putting them together, the Samaritan, from another marginal class, is elevated by Jesus in dignity to that of ideal Jewish women. Hungry after preaching, Jesus invites himself to dinner at the house of a tax collector, yet another marginal class.

In light of all these Scriptures, I am very nervous about all this election-year posturing about the withholding of Communion from Catholic political candidates who hold one position that is contrary to the teachings of the Catholic church, as well as from those who vote for them.

What about those who support a war that the pope doesn't support? What about those who support policies that are economically unjust? What about those who support capital punishment? What about the many other positions of the church? Should we refuse them all and those who vote for them? Who would be left?

I accept our church's right to teach moral positions, and maybe some should not receive Communion. But as unworthy as I am myself, I hope I am never put in the position of having to decide who in the Communion line is worthy and who is not.

Are not our last words, right before we receive Communion, "Lord, I am not worthy to receive you, but only say the word and my soul shall be healed"? After all, even Judas was invited to the Last Supper and given a place of honor, in hopes of a change of heart.

July 15, 2004

Maybe It's Time to Change Your Point of View

Show kindness and compassion toward each other. Zechariah 7:9

People say that you cannot change the past, but you can. You can change the past by changing how you choose to remember it.

You can change the past by looking at it from another point of view. You can change the past by moving from your own point of view to a viewing point. From there you can appreciate not only your own point of view, but other points of view.

The other day, I was going to Brandenburg to preside at the wedding of my niece, Julie. As I traveled out Dixie Highway through Kosmosdale, West Point and Muldraugh, my mind flooded with memories. That was a route I took almost every week as a child. My father was a hard-driving businessman.

Besides his building material business, he always had a few other projects on the side. He owned a couple of farms. He hauled to-bacco and animals to market from there to here, and on the way home, building materials from here to there. To help with securing the chains, the loading and the unloading, my brother Gary and I were required to go along.

I do not have good memories of those trips. But as I drove along that day, I decided not to think of those trips from my point of view, as I have so many times in the past. I tried to think of them from my father's point of view. I started imagining myself balancing seven kids, a new business, paying off two farms, side projects to make a little extra money, and the long, hard days of labor in the hot, sweaty summers and in the cold, freezing days of winter.

I was moved with compassion. Could I have done any better? Probably not. Instead of remembering the glass as half empty, all of a sudden I remember it as being half full.

In the end, the best thing a father and son can say to each other is, "I'm proud of you!" My dad and I could not say that to each other until the last couple of years, and we only said it once, and in a roundabout way. The secret was to move from seeing things from our own point of view to seeing things from each other's point of view.

Bitterness, hard feelings and even hatred are festering wounds that many people carry around with them on a daily basis. People have convinced themselves that they have been wronged and that the only way out is for the one who wronged them to change. More times than not, that never happens, and so they self-righteously hug their poisonous, hard feelings until they become an integral part of their crippled personalities.

Freedom comes, more often than not, when we are able to see things not just from our own point of view, but from the view of the other. From there, compassion is possible.

July 22, 2004

The True Nature of Being "Catholic"

The kingdom of heaven is like a net thrown into the sea, which collects fish of every kind. Matthew 13:47

The word "catholic" means "universal" and "inclusive." One writer says that "catholic" means "here comes everybody."

Though some in our church are growing more and more uncomfortable with concepts such as diversity and inclusiveness, choosing instead to be exclusionary and fundamentalistic, I still like being "catholic."

A few weeks back, I was having breakfast in the dining room at Saint Meinrad Seminary where I now work four days a week. Even though the seminarians had all gone back to their dioceses for the summer, the dining room hummed with activity.

There was a large group of young people, youth leaders in cut-offs and printed tee shirts from parishes all over the country, who were there for youth leadership training. There was a large group of Methodist pastors and lay leaders from central Indiana holding their own conference.

There was an assortment of nuns, priests and brothers from monasteries around the country sharing ideas on church music. There was a small group of Catholic and Protestant seminary students, male and female, who were studying together to be hospital chaplains.

Mingling comfortably in this interesting mixture of diverse groups were two cloistered Carmelite nuns, an elderly widow from New York, a young father and his son, and various seminary faculty members, staff people and kitchen workers. A few monks from the monastery, true to their tradition of hospitality, moved through the crowd encouraging, listening and assisting their guests.

As I surveyed the room, it occurred to me that Jesus would have been proud. He always seemed to have around him an assortment of religious leaders, women, children, soldiers, tax collectors, lepers, demoniacs and a host of other marginal groups. As the Gospel says, "This man welcomes sinners and even eats with them."

I am worried that our church is slowly losing its "catholic" charism to the scared "law and order" people. There seems to be a growing mean-spirited, exclusionary thinking invading our church. To those who would sell our "catholic" charism so as to have a neat little club of cloned robots, I would say: "If it's not messy, it's not real" and "if it's not inclusive, it's not catholic."

Like the parable of the wedding feast of heaven, we in the church are called to go out into the highways and byways and invite the "good and bad alike" to dine with the King. We are the field of weeds and wheat "growing together." We are that "assortment of fish" that God's net drags up from the sea. Because our eyesight and judgment are not too good, it's God's job, not ours, to sort it all out at the end of the day.

To those who are scared by the messiness of today's church, I say: "Trust God. Leave Pope John XXIII's window open. The more the merrier." Personally, I love being "catholic," and I'm proud of it.

July 29, 2004

Some Thoughts about Growing Old

My son, take care of your father when he is old; grieve him not as long as he lives. Even if his mind fails, be considerate with him; revile him not in the fullness of your strength. Sirach 3:12-13

I like old people. I especially like feisty old people, the ones who may be old in body but young at heart. Even as a young priest, I was always more comfortable with the parish senior citizen group than I was with the parish youth group.

Not only am I attracted to the energy of old people, but they also are attracted to my energy. In fact, I have been called an "old lady magnet" more than once to my face. Even Archbishop Kelly pointed out to me that I seem to always have a need for "a mother or two" all the time.

The facts make me have to admit that he is right. I have often found myself knee-deep in "mothers," especially when I was a pastor. Even today one of the highlights of my week is Friday morning, my day off, when I go visit my almost 96-year-old friend.

I am not an expert in "senior citizenry," but I have found out a few things about these "golden years" people. The main thing I have discovered is that many people think all they need is a warm bed, a hot meal, a good bath, a few pills and a hasty visit every few months, when in fact they need what all of us need.

What they really need is to be touched, kissed, hugged, held, appreciated, remembered, recognized, consulted, included, respected and trusted.

I turned 60 this year, so I guess about 10 to 15 years from now I ought to start thinking about getting old myself. I already know what kind of old person I want to be when I get there. I want to be one of those feisty old people myself. I want to be one of those old people I enjoy so much — the kind who choose life, the kind who try new things, the kind who push themselves to be engaged, the kind who are focused on others, the kind who milk life for all it's worth.

I sort of look forward to the day when I no longer feel the need to fix everything, but can simply enjoy everything — the day when I can stir up stuff and get away with it; the day when people will think I am cute for doing it.

I agree with Norman Cousins, who said, "Death is not the greatest loss in life. The greatest loss is what dies within us while we live." While I am I admiring those senior citizens who choose to live no matter how old they get, I am learning from them. They are teaching me not to be one of those about whom Nicholas Murray Butler spoke when he said, "Many people's tombstones should read, "Died at 30. Buried at 60.""

August 5, 2004

Wasting Energy on Things that Don't Matter

No one who puts his hand to the plow and keeps looking back is fit for the kingdom of God. Luke 9

Have you ever been sitting at a table pouring your heart out to someone and notice that they keep focusing over your shoulder on other people in the room? Have you ever made an appointment with a doctor or salesperson and had the meeting interrupted, over and over again, by their intercoms, cell phones or knocks on the door? Do you remember how discounted you felt?

Some of you know what it's like to be married to a spouse with a roaming eye, what a famous old country song calls, "being married and acting single." Others of you know what it's like being in a relationship with someone who is not really committed, someone who is still open to "the latest best offer" — what another song calls "loving you 'til the right one comes along."

You know how used and unimportant it makes you feel. Words come to mind, such as "half-hearted, distracted, preoccupied, lukewarm, indifferent, perfunctory, disinterested, inattentive, uncommitted, neglectful and unfocused."

In the Gospel story from which the above citation is taken, there are four less than committed responses to Jesus' call to follow him. The Samaritans would not even listen to the invitation because Jesus was Jewish. Jews and Samaritans, as a rule, hated each other and had nothing to do with each other.

The second response represents those who say "yes" enthusiastically, but who do not have the intestinal fortitude to carry through.

The third response represents those who promise to "get around to" answering the call "someday." The fourth response represents those who say "yes" to the call, but try to "squeeze it in," as if their new life can somehow be added to their old life without having to change anything.

My friends, it is especially hard today for disciples to keep our focus on what is truly important when the Catholic church in the United States is so dysfunctional. It is so easy to get distracted and get off course.

Personally, I am really tired of all the hoopla over "wine pouring," "Communion withholding" and "liberal-conservative culture wars" in our church. Jesus called it "straining out gnats and swallowing camels." I am tired of wasting energy on little things that don't really matter while the big needs of the church go unnoticed.

The temptation is to look around for other options. The answer, of course, is to stay the course. This is the time, I believe, for us to focus on the essentials of our faith, to focus on the treasure and not the crock that holds it; to focus on faithful discipleship and not get too caught up in the petty little side issues that some are trying to pass off as "essential"; to focus on holding the discipleship plow firmly on course no matter what is happening behind us, beside us or in front of us and without waiting for a "better day" or "better field" to plow.

August 12, 2004

A Car Crash and a Wake-Up Call

You also must be prepared, for at an hour
you do not expect, the Son of Man will
come. Luke 12: 40

We never know when our time is up. Many of us imagine, even wish for, an unconscious death when we are old and sick. But for some of us, our lives can be over in a flash.

Most of us believe in the Woody Allen quote, "I know everybody dies, but I'm still hoping that an exception might be made in my case." Just because we own an IRA and we have paid into Social Security, there's no guarantee that we will be around to spend it.

Recently, the thought of my own death was once again shoved into my consciousness when my car was struck from the rear in Brandenburg, Kentucky. Miraculously, no one was seriously hurt, but both his truck and mine were totaled. As I watched the other truck speeding toward me through my rear-view mirror, I had time to realize that I was either going to die, be crippled or be spared. After it was over, it slowly dawned on me that, for some reason, it was not my time to go.

It was my second automobile wake-up call. About 15 years ago when I lived downtown, my car was broad-sided in the driver's door by a man who tried to outrun a red light. Again, no one was hurt, but once more, my truck was totally destroyed after all the windows broke out and it rolled over. With all the doors crushed shut, the firemen had to get me out through the back window.

Both wrecks involved books. When the wreck downtown was over, I noticed my copy of Lazarus, a novel by Morris West, had been thrown out into the street. As it waved its pages at me in the breeze, the fact that Lazarus was the man Jesus raised from the dead was not lost on me.

When the Brandenburg wreck was over, I noticed about a hundred blue hymnals strewn about on the road, hymnals that I was transporting in the back of my truck. As they caught my attention, I immediately remembered that my theme song as a priest for the last 34 years has been, "How Can I Keep From Singing?"

All this might sound ridiculously sentimental to some, but for those of us who have a simple faith in God's providence, these wake-up calls deliver a message. Those of us who have survived a plane crash, car wreck or even a cancer scare all have the same realization: our purpose here has not ended, and we ought to live more consciously.

The message for me, underneath all of this, is that "we know not the day or the hour" and therefore we should "make hay while the sun shines." Like pregnant women days away from delivery, we need to live with a bag packed. That does not mean we need to be obsessed with death. It does mean, however, that we should be obsessed about life. The best way to be prepared for death is to live well.

August 19, 2004

God Wants Us to Have
Everything We Need

Jesus was praying in a certain place, and when
He had finished, one of his disciples said to
him, "Lord, teach us to pray." Luke 11

When I was a seminarian at the old St. Thomas Seminary on
Brownsboro Road, we were forever saying prayers. We got up at 6
a.m. for morning prayers. In my heart, I didn't believe God wanted to
be bothered that early in the morning, but I kept it to myself, because I didn't want to be reprimanded for being a heathen.

After morning prayer, we went to Mass. We prayed before and
after every breakfast, lunch, supper, study hall and class. We read
from Scripture and the lives of the saints. After supper, we prayed
the rosary. Last of all, we had night prayers and went to bed at 9:20
p.m. sharp.

In between all this, there was Benediction, Stations of the Cross,
retreats and holy hours. We were expected to do some personal
prayer on our own. We even prayed at sports events. Frankly, I think
God was tired of hearing from us.

If it hadn't been for the '60s, I might have turned against God
altogether. Seminary in the late '60s was a lot less structured. We
had our basic routine, but they left some of the styles of praying up
to us. Until then, I always thought that I was spiritually defective
because some of those old prayer forms didn't seem to fit me.

Today, we have a beautiful passage about prayer. It contains
some very simple and basic truths about Christian prayer.

The first thing Jesus talks about is the kind of God to whom we pray. Jesus invites us to address God with the affectionate word "abba," in English "dadda." Addressing God with baby talk was a shock to the people of his day. They were much more comfortable with euphemisms, like "most high" or "holy one." The actual name of God was far too holy to be pronounced aloud.

The second thing he taught was that we do not have to plead and beg like a neighbor in need of bread at midnight. Our God, our "dadda," already wants us to have everything we need.

The third thing Jesus teaches us about prayer is that when we ask for something, we will not be given things that merely look good to us, but only those things that are actually good for us. Like good parents, who do not give their children everything they cry for, especially those things that will hurt them, God will not give us things that are bad for us.

If we really believe that God is like a doting parent, who wants us to have the best but protects us from things that are not good for us, then prayer becomes very simple. All we have to do is ask, hold our hands out and wait. If we don't get it, we can trust that it is either not good for us or the time is not right.

August 26, 2004

Crossing the Desert Is
Part of the Journey

The whole community grumbled against Moses and Aaron, saying, "Would that we had died at the Lord's hand in the land of Egypt, as we sat by our fleshpots and ate our fill of bread! But you had to lead us into the desert to make the whole community die of famine." Exodus 16:2,3

The story of Exodus offers us a helpful map for any process of transition and transformation, be it for institutions in general or for individuals in particular. The Exodus experience seems to have four movements: a setting out in excitement, a period of disillusionment, a call to perseverance and, finally, a time of integration.

When Moses led the people out of Egypt toward the Promised Land, they left their old life with images of "milk and honey" dancing in their heads. Not too long into their journey, they hit a desert. A desert is a place of hunger, thirst and danger, an unfamiliar place of uncertainty and doubt.

Worn out by the stress of being "in between," they complain and yearn for "the flesh pots of Egypt," the "good old days." They want to go back to what was familiar. Moses, who had the duty of keeping hope alive, keeps prodding them to "go on." Finally, after 40 years of wandering, they see the Promised Land on the horizon and finally move into it.

Our church is on this journey as we speak. Those of us who were around for Vatican Council II remember the excitement and euphoria of setting out to build a renewed church. Like the Israelites, we did not count on a desert experience; we thought it was going to be easy. Sick of the confusion and disorientation, there are those who are grumbling against Pope John XXII and those who led us out, yearning for "the good old days" before the council.

Like Israelites with their selective memory, these people idealize our past and would have us go back as an answer to their discomfort. Our wisest leaders, however, know that a "desert" is part of the deal and bid us to keep going, knowing that what was begun by the Holy Spirit will be brought to completion.

Excitement, disillusionment, perseverance and, finally, integration are part of every transition, be it the remodeling a house, the path to sobriety, a new marriage, an abused spouse leaving her abuser, a church in the process of renewal or a priest moving into another assignment. "With each passage of human growth, we must shed a protective structure (like a hardy crustacean). We are left exposed and vulnerable — but also yeasty and embryonic again, capable of stretching in ways we hadn't known before." (Gail Sheehy)

Every person going through a major change should expect a "desert" along the way. It's part of the process. When they hit that "desert," and they will, they should not conclude that they have made a mistake. By conquering our "deserts," by remaining faithful, we will move into that new life that we used to imagine.

September 2, 2004

Can You Keep Walking with God?

Faith is the realization of what is hoped for and the evidence of things not seen.
Hebrews 11:1

I have been at this "priest thing" almost all of my life. I have never really wanted to be anything else. I first felt "called" when I was seven years old, and I started seminary at age 14. I was ordained at 26.

I have been a priest now for 34 years. Last year, for the first time in my life, I actually thought about quitting. I was so angry, disappointed, embarrassed and disillusioned that I thought about throwing in the towel, moving out of state and finding a job that had nothing to do with God, the church or priesthood. I wanted to quit, but I didn't. I can't.

The question I kept coming back to was this one: "Where is my faith placed?" Is my faith in priests? No! Is it in bishops? No! Is it in the pope? No! They are merely "earthenware jars." They hold the "treasure," but they are not the "treasure." Is it in organized religion? No! Organized religion has and will always be in need of reform.

I finally came to this conclusion: to leave would be to turn my back on God. How could I turn my back on the God who called me to be a priest simply because the going is rough? How could I go off and leave my "faith family" in its time of need?

After exploring the possibility of leaving, wallowing in my depression and wrestling with the question of faith, I finally came to the realization that if I have faith at all, then this is the time to prove it — by staying and remaining faithful.

Do you have faith? No, I don't mean do you believe that this or that Bible story happened or this or that church doctrine to be true. I mean, do you really trust God? Can you keep walking with God, even when you can't see where you are going, even when your most precious things, relationships and assumptions are taken away from you?

I am amazed at people who say they have "lost their faith" when a church is renovated, an altar rail is removed, a Mass time is changed, a school is closed or a church member disappoints them. If faith only holds up when things are going fine, when the world is the way we like it, when we are blessed with all that life has to offer, when every church member is perfect, then it is not faith.

Is your faith being tested? Here is how you will know if you have passed the test. If we can go on loving and trusting God after we hear the diagnosis of cancer, after our house burns down, after we lose our job, after our spouse dies and after our friends abandon us — after we lose everything we can lose — then we can say we have faith.

September 9, 2004

We Need to Use the "Medicine of Mercy"

While he was at table in his house, many tax collectors and sinners sat with Jesus and his disciples; for there were many who followed him. Mark 2:15

Judgment and condemnation drive people out of the church. Compassion and forgiveness bring them in. This has been made abundantly clear to me, both from both my reading of the Gospels and from my own personal experience as a pastor.

Some of the most beautiful parables of Jesus were given in response to those who were big on judgment and condemnation. Both Jesus and the Pharisees hated sin, but they disagreed on what to do about it. The Pharisees chose judgment and condemnation. Jesus chose compassion and forgiveness. Sinners fled from the Pharisees and flocked to Jesus.

Through a series of personal conversion experiences, I have come to believe that the "universal and unconditional love of God" is the "good news." I stumbled onto it like a person would stumble on a buried treasure. It was transforming.

I had believed that God's love for us was conditional on our success in keeping the rules. I had mistakenly assumed that God loves us when we are good, quits loving us when we are bad and starts loving us again when we shape up. What I had failed to realize was the fact that God loves us even while we are sinners.

In the parable of the loving father, the father loves the older son who stayed home and kept the rules, but he also loves the son who lived with the pigs.

In the parable of the vineyard workers, the owner of the vineyard gives all his workers a full day's pay, no matter when they started working. In the parable of the lost sheep, the shepherd certainly loves the 99 who do what sheep are supposed to do, but he also loves the sheep who wandered off. In the parable of the wedding feast, the good and bad alike are invited to be part of the wedding party.

When I was the pastor of the Cathedral of the Assumption from 1983 to 1997, I made a conscious decision to preach this "good news." We grew dramatically. I got a lot of credit — too much credit, in fact. What drew them was not the messenger but the message.

I am troubled by what I see as a mean spirit invading our church, disguised as a crusade for "truth." I agree with their goal, but I reject their methods. They are driving more people out of the church than they will ever bring in. Unable to inspire people to holiness, they are settling for naming sins and condemning sinners. Their harsh condemnation may make them feel righteous, but it doesn't turn many people around.

I like what Pope John XXIII said when he opened Vatican Council II. He said that "nowadays the church prefers to make use of the medicine of mercy rather than severity." The "medicine of mercy" works. "Severity" doesn't.

September 16, 2004

Humility is Often Misunderstood

Whoever exalts himself will be humbled,
but the one who humbles himself will be
exalted. Luke 14:11

Humility is not a popular virtue these days. Maybe it is because so many of us are reacting to an understanding of humility that borders on humiliation.

Humility, rightly understood, is a virtue. Humiliation is psychological abuse. Humility is about being who you are, no more and no less. Humiliation is about being destructive to your dignity and self-respect.

Humility is certainly not about pretending to be something greater than you are, but neither is it about pretending to be less than you are. Humility is about accepting the truth about yourself, the whole truth.

Human beings have always had a problem with humility — being who they really are — without exaggeration or diminishment. The problem goes all the way back to Adam and Eve. An African-American Baptist minister, who spoke on the Book of Genesis at one of my graduations, said it best: "God has always been happy being God. The plants and animals have always been happy being plants and animals. But human beings have never been happy being who they are. They want to be God one day and animals the next."

Most of us know that we can sin against humility by being proud, inflating our worth, our talents or our abilities beyond the truth. However, I believe a bigger problem than pride is sinning against humility by trying to get ourselves and others to believe that we are less than we really are.

Humility is not about putting ourselves down but about accepting our light, our strengths and our talents. Jesus said, "Let your light shine so that people can see your good deeds [here is where humility comes in] so that, seeing your good deeds, they may give glory to God." Humility is about accepting what God gave us and using it, not to exalt ourselves, but so that God will be exalted. "No one lights a lamp and then covers it over with a bushel basket. It belongs on a lamp stand."

Pride is about presenting something about ourselves that is false. Humility is about presenting something about ourselves that is true. Pride is a lie. Humility is truth.

I think this quote from Marianne Williamson — a quote used by Nelson Mandela in his first inaugural speech as the first black president of South Africa — says what true humility is all about:

"Our deepest fear is not that we are inadequate. Our deepest fear is that we are powerful beyond measure.

"It is our light, not our darkness, that most frightens us. We ask ourselves, who am I to be brilliant, gorgeous, talented and fabulous?

"You are a child of God. Your playing small doesn't serve the world. There is nothing enlightened about shrinking so that other people won't feel insecure around us.

"We were born to make manifest the glory of God that is within us."

September 23, 2004